Elite • 194

The Chinese People's Liberation Army since 1949

Ground Forces

BENJAMIN LAI

ILLUSTRATED BY ADAM HOOK
Series editor Martin Windrow

First published in Great Britain in 2012 by Osprey Publishing,
Midland House, West Way, Botley, Oxford, OX2 0PH, UK
44-02 23rd Street, Suite 219, Long Island City, NY 11101, USA

E-mail: info@ospreypublishing.com

OSPREY PUBLISHING IS PART OF THE OSPREY GROUP

A CIP catalog record for this book is available from the British Library

Print ISBN: 978 1 78096 056 2
PDF ebook ISBN: 978 1 78096 057 9
ePub ebook ISBN: 978 1 78200 320 5

Editor: Martin Windrow
Index by Rob Munro
Typeset in Sabon and Myriad Pro
Originated by PDQ Digital Media Solutions, Bungay, UK

Printed in Hong Kong through Worldprint Ltd

12 13 14 15 16 10 9 8 7 6 5 4 3 2 1

Osprey Publishing is supporting the Woodland Trust, the UK's leading
woodland conservation charity, by funding the dedication of trees.

www.ospreypublishing.com

DEDICATION

To my daughter, Faith Ying Lai

AUTHOR'S NOTE

To accord with common English-language usage, the PLA is described in
the text as the "Chinese People's Liberation Army," but in captions to the
actual Chinese script – e.g. on badges – it is correctly rendered as "China
PLA" (Zhōngguó Rénmín Jiěfàngjūn). The majority of Chinese names in this
book are Romanized using the Hanyu Pinyin system, the International ISO
standard for Chinese transliteration. A few names are retained in the old
Yale Romanization style, due to their familiarity in the English-speaking
world – e.g. Taipei, the capital of Taiwan; Chiang Kaishek, the leader of China
during World War II; and the Vietnamese leader, Ho Chi Minh.

ACKNOWLEDGMENTS

I would like to thank Benjamin Lee for the opportunity to visit the PLA Hong
Kong Garrison base on the 2011 Chinese National Day; and Ms Bonnie
Leung, for her help with photo editing work, which contributed greatly to
the interest of this book.

Apart from those taken by the author personally, the photographs
reproduced here are from Chinese military publications and open internet
sources.

ARTIST'S NOTE

Readers may care to note that the original paintings from which the color
plates in this book were prepared are available for private sale. All
reproduction copyright whatsoever is retained by the Publishers. All
enquiries should be addressed to:

Scorpio, 158 Mill Road, Hailsham, East Sussex BN27 2SH, UK

scorpiopaintings@btinternet.com

The Publishers regret that they can enter into no correspondence upon this
matter.

Acronyms used in this text:

AAU	Army Aviation Unit	KMT	Kuomintang (Nationalist Party of China)
AGL	automatic grenade launcher	LRRP	long range reconnaissance patrol
AMS	Academy of Military Science	LSW	light support weapon (squad-level light machine gun)
APC	armored personnel carrier	LVT	landing vehicle, tracked
ARV	armored recovery vehicle	MBRL	multi-barrel rocket launcher
ATGM	antitank guided missile	MBT	main battle tank
CMC	Central Military Commission	MD	Military District
CT	counter-terrorist	MI	Motorized Infantry
ERA	explosive reactive armor	MPS	Ministry of Public Security
GAD	General Armament Department	MR	Military Region
GLD	General Logistic Department	MRs	Motor Rifles
GMLB	Guided Missile Launcher Brigade	MSD	Military Sub-District
GPD	General Political Department	MSS	Ministry of State Security
GSD	General Staff Department	NDU	National Defense University
ICBM	inter-continental ballistic missile	NUDT	National University of Defense Technology
IFV	infantry fighting vehicle	PAP	People's Armed Police
JNCO	junior non-commissioned officer	PAVN	People's Army of Viet Nam

PCG	personal combat gear
PLA	People's Liberation Army (according to context, either ground forces, or all three armed services)
PLA/AF	People's Liberation Army/Air Force
PLA/N	People's Liberation Army/Navy
PRC	People's Republic of China
QRF	quick reaction force
RRU	rapid reaction unit
SAC	Second Artillery Corps, PLA (strategic nuclear strike force)
SACLOS	semi-automatic command to line of sight (second generation AT missiles, requiring the operator to keep the crosshairs on the target throughout flight of weapon)
SF	special forces
SNCO	senior non-commissioned officer
SPATG	self-propelled antitank gun
SPG	self-propelled gun
SWAT	special weapons and tactics

CONTENTS

INTRODUCTION   4
Origins of the PLA

CHRONOLOGY & KEY EVENTS   6
Foundation of the People's Republic, 1949 ▪ The 1950s: the Korean War, 1950–53 – final clashes with the Nationalists – Burma – Tibet – the French Indochina War, 1950–54 ▪ The 1960s: the Vietnam War, 1965–72 – the Indian border clash, 1962 – onset of the Cultural Revolution, 1967 – Sino-Soviet border skirmishes, 1969 ▪ The 1970s: the Sino-Vietnamese War, 1979 ▪ The 1980s: renewed Sino-Vietnamese hostilities, 1980 & 1984–91 – consequences of the Tiananmen Square incident, 1989 ▪ The 1990s to date: first PLA deployments with UN forces – takeover of Hong Kong and Macau – the 2008 natural disasters

THE PLA TODAY   18
Quasi-military roles ▪ Organization: chain of command ▪ Regular units ▪ Reserve units ▪ People's Armed Police ▪ Militia ▪ General Headquarters departments ▪ Senior-level military academies ▪ Military Regions and local commands

CURRENT TACTICAL ORGANIZATION   28
Unit identification ▪ Organization, squad to battalion ▪ Organization, regiment and above ▪ Readiness classifications

SOME KEY COMBAT ARMS   38
Army Aviation ▪ Armor ▪ Special Forces: PLA groups – PAP "Snow Leopard" Commando Unit ▪ Airborne force ▪ Strategic strike force: Second Artillery Corps

PERSONNEL   49
Recruitment and training ▪ The NCOs ▪ The officers ▪ PLA academies ▪ Uniformed civilian personnel

UNIFORMS & COMBAT EQUIPMENT   52
Service dress: PLA – PAP ▪ Combat dress and equipment

SELECT BIBLIOGRAPHY   63

INDEX   64

THE CHINESE PEOPLE'S LIBERATION ARMY SINCE 1949
GROUND FORCES

INTRODUCTION

The Chinese People's Liberation Army (Zhōngguó Rénmín Jiěfàngjūn – hereafter, PLA) is the armed wing of the Chinese Communist Party (CCP). It traces its origins to the Red Army of Workers and Peasants (Gōngnóng Hóngjūn) that was established by the Nánchāng Uprising of August 1, 1927 by men of the Kuomintang army's 24th Division led by General (later Field Marshal) Zhū Dé. August 1 is still regarded as "PLA Day" in China, and the emblems of the PLA still bear the Chinese characters for 8 (Bā) and 1 (Yī), recalling the first day of the eighth month.

In the mid-1920s the Chinese communists were cooperating with the then-dominant political force in the country, the Nationalist Party (Kuomintang, KMT) led by Chiang Kaishek (Jiǎng Jièshí), against various regional warlord armies.[1] A series of disputes resulted in a split between the CCP and KMT, and the first battle between them in August 1927. The Nánchāng Uprising saw the defeat of the pro-communist troops; Zhū Dé then led them in a retreat to Jǐnggāng Mountain, where they were joined by another defeated rag-tag army from the failed Autumn Harvest Uprising, led by Máo Zédōng. To crush this communist guerrilla force the KMT established a series of encirclements, but the Red Army eventually broke out, and in October 1934 embarked on their historic "Long March" that was to end a year later in the mountainous desert plateaux of Yánān. These soon became a CCP-controlled zone and stronghold, despite continuous pressure from the Nationalist Army.

However, the Japanese invasion of northeast China in 1931, and the 1937 Marco Polo Bridge Incident, prompted the creation of a temporary "united front" by the CCP and KMT against the Japanese (though this truce was not universally observed by either side). During this time, the CCP established the Eighth Route Army and the New Fourth Army; instead of preying on the peasants like the armies of old, these forces drew support from the rural populations, and were able rapidly to expand their areas of control beyond Yánān. The KMT was soon faced with a two-front war – on the one hand fighting the Japanese, on the other hand having to divert resources to contain the CCP's ever-expanding influence over large areas of rural China.

The current PLA Ground Forces cap badge, Model 07 uniform. Note the Chinese characters for "8" above "1" on the red star. (Author's photo)

1 See Osprey Men-at-Arms 463, *Chinese Warlord Armies 1911–30*

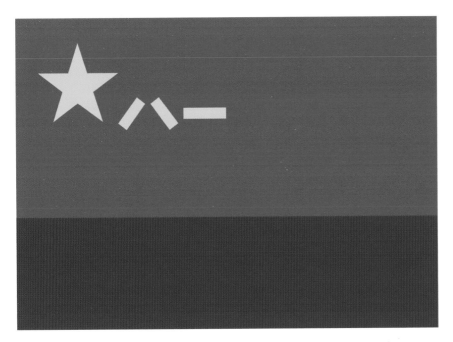

The end of World War II in the Pacific in 1945 saw the start of the Chinese Civil War proper, and the "Red" Army was then renamed as the Chinese People's Liberation Army. It was able to take advantage of large quantities of leftover Japanese weapons and ordnance, and consequently its military capability expanded considerably, to include for the first time large-caliber artillery and tanks. The PLA progressed from guerrilla tactics to set-piece battles, such as the campaigns of Liáoníng/Shěnyáng (Líaoshên Zhànyì, 1948), Huáihǎi (Huáihǎi Zhànyì, 1948), and Běijīng/Tianjin (Píngjīn Zhànyì, 1949). These campaigns, in which the PLA destroyed 173 KMT divisions and eliminated some 1.5 million Nationalist troops, essentially sealed the victory of the CCP. In September 1949, Chiang Kaishek escaped to the island of Taiwan with some two million supporters; he proclaimed Taipei as the temporary capital of the Republic of China, and continued to assert his government as the sole legitimate authority over all of China. On the mainland, the CCP, with Máo Zédōng at the helm, established the People's Republic of China (PRC) on October 1, 1949.[2]

In the more than half-century since then, the PLA has expanded from an ill-equipped, ground-only army into combined armed forces that include a potent nuclear capability and steadily growing naval and air services. In the early days the PLA drew its support from the Soviet Union and developed largely along Soviet lines; however, the split between the two communist powers in the mid-1960s saw China begin to embark on a self-modernization program, eventually acquiring equipment originating in Israel, the United States, Russia, Ukraine and France. Since the "opening" of China in the early 1980s the country's economic success has also given the PLA a long-awaited opportunity to modernize its bloated organization, demobilizing almost a million soldiers in 1985. By the first decade of the 21st century the PLA has been transformed from a largely conscript army modeled on Soviet lines into an increasingly professional force more comparable to Western models.

2 See MAA 306, *Chinese Civil War Armies 1911–49*

October 1, 1949: PLA soldiers march past during the first National Day parade in Tiananmen Square, Běijīng. They wear captured Japanese steel helmets, and are armed with Czech-made ZB vz 26 light machine guns; at this date the PLA had a motley armory of Japanese weapons and those taken from the Chinese KMT, including Czech, US and even some British small arms. Note that they are marching in a conventional cadence – the Soviet-style "goose-step" had not yet been adopted. (*China Magazine*)

CHRONOLOGY & KEY EVENTS

1949, October 1 Establishment of the People's Republic of China.
1949, October 25–27 PLA attempt to control Jīnmén island (a.k.a. Quemoy) is thwarted in battle of Gǔníngtóu (Gǔníngtóu Zhīyì or Jīnmén Zhīyì).

THE 1950s:
The Korean War, 1950–53
In October 1950 the Chinese People's Volunteer Army (PVA) entered the Korean War in support of North Korea, and its battle-hardened troops rapidly gained successes against the UN forces. As the war drew on, however, the lack of cold-weather protection and effective air cover, and weaknesses in firepower, caused the PVA to suffer severely. Despite material setbacks the PVA was able to hold the much superior UN forces to a stalemate, culminating in an armistice in July 1953. According to Chinese sources, China committed 1.9 million soldiers to Korea plus another half-million as combat replacements, giving a total of 2.4 million over the three years of the war. (If militias, mostly in rear areas, are included, the grand total of those serving during this period rises to 3 million).[3]

Chinese casualties were reported as 115,786 combat deaths, 221,264 combat injuries, and 29,085 captured, giving a total of 366,135. Non-combat casualties to the PVA were as high as an additional 556,146; however, of the many that were hospitalized 173,405 eventually returned to active duty, reducing final non-combat losses to 382,741. Accidental deaths accounted for 10,808; 73,686 were deemed unsuitable and returned to civilian duties; 786 committed suicide, 64 were executed, 3,089 were imprisoned for criminal activities, 450 dismissed, 17,715 went AWOL, and 4,202 died of illness.

3 See MAA 174, *The Korean War 1950–53*

Final clashes with the Nationalists

For most of the 1950s the PLA was almost continuously engaged in mopping-up operations against the remnants of the Nationalist Army. In 1950 the PLA completed the conquest of Hǎinán Island (Hǎinándǎo), the battle of the Wànshān archipelago (Wànshān Qúndǎo Zhīyì), and the retaking of Zhōushān Island (Zhōushāndǎo). In 1952 the PLA won the battle of the Nanpeng archipelago, and in 1953 the Dongshan Island campaign (Dongshān Qúndǎo Zhīyì). By 1955 the Yǐjiāngshān Island campaign (Yǐjiāngshāndǎo Zhīyì) saw the elimination of the last significant KMT forces from offshore China, bar the islands of Jīnmén and Mǎzǔ. The Jīnmén artillery duels (Jīnmén Páozhàn) across the strait of Quemoy lasted for some 20 years, though they were at their most intense between August and October 1958. (Between late 1958 and 1979 both sides scaled down the military contest into a political demonstration that eventually became farcical, with both sides agreeing to only shoot on alternate days, deliberately aiming at unmanned zones to minimize casualties. By the 1970s most of the shells contained only propaganda leaflets.)

英雄黄继光

Propaganda poster depicting a PLA hero of the Korean War – Huáng Jìguāng (1930–52), who was posthumously awarded the title of Hero Special Class for his conduct in the Battle of Triangle Hill (in Chinese, Shǎng Gān Líng) in October 1952. Huang wears Model 50 PLA uniform, but the People's Volunteer Army in Korea actually fought with all insignia removed. (*China* Magazine)

Burma and Tibet

Supported by the CIA, surviving KMT troops escaped to Burma, where these diehards continued the struggle in the Sino-Burmese frontier zone between 1950 and 1961. By the 1970s support for their guerrilla campaign was dwindling, and in order to survive some turned to opium cultivation, creating the infamous Golden Triangle. By the 1980s many of these old soldiers and their descendents had tired of a criminal/guerrilla lifestyle and took advantage of an amnesty to settle in Taiwan, although some chose to stay in Thailand to this day.

October 1959 saw a CIA-inspired and supported uprising by exile Tibetans; this Lhasa Uprising was quickly crushed by the PLA, although sporadic guerrilla attacks by Tibetan exiles continued into the early 1960s.

The French Indochina War

For more than 25 years, China provided military, economic and political support to communist Vietnam. Late in 1949 Ho Chi Minh, the leader of the communist Viet Minh resistance to French postwar reoccupation, asked China for assistance. In response China formed a military advisory group (CMAG), and 281 military and political officers crossed the frontier into North Vietnam incognito. They were headed by Gen Wéi Guóqīng, and Máo's personal representative Gen Chén Gēng – the latter chosen because he knew Ho from his days at Whampoa Military Academy. China took on the missions of arming and training Vietnamese troops in camps established inside China, and of advising them within North Vietnam. Under direct orders from Máo, the CMAG was to allow the Vietnamese to take all the glory from any consequent military successes.

An historic photo dating from 1950–51, showing the PLA's General Chén Gēng (second from left, round spectacles) with a youthful-looking Vo Nguyen Giap (third from left), commander of the People's Army of Vietnam.

With this help, Gen Vo Nguyen Giap's People's Army of Vietnam (PAVN) was able to expand its main force to seven divisions by 1954, including an artillery division. To sustain this effort the PLA military support team would expand to more than 15,000 men, including substantial numbers of logistic, technical, tactical and political advisors attached at all levels of the PAVN command structure. General Chén provided key input in the development of the master plan that forced the French to evacuate Lào Cai, Cao Bang, Lang Son, and Hoa Binh, abandoning virtually all of Vietnam north of the Red

A

THE 1950s
(1) Field Marshal Peng De Huai, Model 55 generals' dress uniform

Field Marshal Peng De Huai (1898–1974) was the commander-in-chief of the People's Volunteer Army in the Korean War, and Defense Minister from 1954 to 1959. The Model 55 general officer's dress uniform was modeled on the Soviet Army equivalent of April 1945, in a dark "sea green" with red piping and gold "Russia braid" on the collar and cuffs. Note the gold oakleaf wreath around the cap badge, gold chin cords, a gold star and oakleaf spray on the collar, a larger star above the cuff piping and braid, and a line of oakleaves around the cuffs. The gold braid shoulder boards show red edging except at the outer end; they bear marshal's ranking of a large gold and red national crest centered, and a large silver star. Marshal Peng displays on his right breast the stars of three decorations: (top to bottom) PLA "8.1" Medal 1st Class, Independence and Freedom Medal 1st Class, and Liberation Medal 1st Class.

(2) Sergeant, infantry, Model 55 field uniform

The summer-weight Model 55 field uniform was made in a number of hues by dispersed factories, often this yellowish-green drab shade. Officers had four internal jacket pockets, with "bracket"-shaped flaps on the chest and straight flaps below the waist; enlisted men had the breast pockets only. This uniform included a sidecap resembling the Soviet *pilotka*, which was very unpopular. The only insignia are the small Model 55 PLA badge on the cap, and collar patches. The latter are in the PLA's red, with (for enlisted ranks) silver metal pin-on insignia, overlaying (for NCOs) a single yellow stripe; three stars denote the rank of sergeant. His simple bandolier equipment is made from canvas, and holds clips

of ammunition for his 7.62mm Type 56 semiautomatic rifle – the Chinese copy of the Soviet Simonov SKS, with a folding cruciform-section spike bayonet.

(3) Corporal Lei Feng, Transport Corps, Model 55 winter uniform

Lei Feng (1940–62) was a driver JNCO in the Transport Corps who was killed in a traffic accident. He was posthumously selected as the perfect model of a communist citizen, and was made the subject of a propaganda campaign initiated by Máo, the youth of the country being exhorted to "Learn from Comrade Lei Feng." He wears the padded green winter version of the Model 55 uniform, with a brown fur-flapped cap resembling the Soviet *ushanka*. His collar patches with two silver stars and a "head-on car" badge identify his rank and corps, and he displays a gold "Máo" pin above a commemorative badge on the left breast (this latter is not an official medal). He is armed with the 7.62mm Type 54 submachine gun – the Chinese copy of the folding-butt Soviet PPS-43. A brown leather four-pocket magazine pouch is slung from his right shoulder on a webbing strap, held steady by his leather waist belt.

1950s insignia:

(4) Model 55 PLA Police collar patch, sergeant. This design was in use by the forerunners of today's PAP from November 26, 1955 to December 31, 1958. The officer's version had the Police shield, but no stars or yellow stripe; the general officer's patch had yellow edging.

(5) Model 58 PLA Ground Forces collar patch, captain. This design was in use from January 18, 1958 to May 31, 1965. All officer ranks had the yellow edging on three sides.

(6) Model 55 PLA Ground Forces daily dress shoulder board, lieutenant

(7) Model 55 PLA cap badge

River Delta by the end of 1950.[4] In June 1951 Gen Chén was recalled to China, and that August he was appointed deputy commander of the Chinese PVA in Korea; thereafter Gen Wéi bore the sole responsibility for advising the PAVN.

The signing of the Korean armistice in July 1953 allowed even greater resources to be devoted to supporting the Vietnamese struggle. China's material support, always substantial, was to reach as much as 4,000 tons a month just before the battle of Dien Bien Phu in early 1954, and included significant numbers of US 105mm howitzers captured in Korea. Simultaneously, new cadres of battle-hardened PLA officers fresh from Korea arrived to give invaluable assistance during the preparations for that climactic battle. ("Cadre" is a communist term often used in reference to those in command – whether officers in the PLA, or managers in factories.) It was the CMAG, drawing upon hard-learned lessons from Korea, who insisted that all artillery must be hidden in shellproof dugouts, which proved to be the battle-winning factor at Dien Bien Phu. Two battalions equipped with "recoilless rifles" and MBRLs were sent south; to counter French airpower China also furnished the PAVN with four battalions of AA troops equipped with 37mm guns, and engineering experts were sent to assist in the construction of hundreds of miles of siege and communication trenches. On the victorious conclusion of the battle of Dien Bien Phu in May 1954 the CMAG ended its mission in Vietnam, but Chinese military aid continued to flow.

THE 1960s:
The Vietnam War

When the North Vietnamese faced major intervention by the US in their war against South Vietnam, they once again asked China for help, and this time China participated directly with combat support troops such as AA, truck and railway units as well as engineering and construction troops. From August 1965 to March 1968 alone, more than 15,000 PLA troops entered North Vietnam, participating in 2,153 direct engagements, and shooting down 1,707 aircraft and helicopters.

All in all, during the whole war some 320,000 PLA troops would serve in Vietnam in various capacities. The largest category were AA troops, numbering some 150,000 men with 16 divisions' worth of air defense assets. China also sent some 100,000 PLA construction and engineering troops; during the war they were responsible for building or repairing 1,778 railroad facilities, 577km (358 miles) of railroad tracks, 1,206km (749 miles) of major roads, 305 bridges, 4,441 underground shelters, two military airfields with associated hardened shelters, 9 harbors, 123 underground military facilities, 103km (64 miles) of undersea communication cables, and 5 petroleum pipelines totaling 159km (99 miles). The third largest group were the 2nd and 13th Divisions of the Railroad Corps, a specialist PLA troop category responsible for rail transport and maintenance of railroad facilities. Entering Vietnam from 1965, these troops were formed into two specialist corps, Nos. 1 and 6; later rotations brought the 12th Div, 58th Regt and 10th Independent Regt of the Railroad Corps to Vietnam. In the eight years 1965–72 the PLA in Vietnam suffered 5,270 casualties, of whom 1,070 were killed.

4 See MAA 322, *The French Indochina War 1946–54*

In addition to direct involvement, China also provided free training for more than 6,000 Vietnamese cadres, and facilitated the delivery of military aid from other communist countries, transported via the Trans-Siberian railway and delivered into Vietnam by the PLA Transport Corps. According to Vietnamese sources, North Vietnam received 160 million tons of aid from China, of which 93.3 percent was free of charge. This total included 2.2 million rifles and machine guns; 74,000 artillery pieces; 1.2 billion rounds of small arms ammunition; 18.7 million artillery rounds; 176 naval vessels; 170 aircraft; 552 tanks and 320 APCs; 16,000 trucks; 3 surface/air missile battalions and 180 SA-2 missiles; 2 radar systems; 2 pontoon bridges; 18,240 tons of explosives; 1 million sets of radio and telephone equipment; 130 tons of diesel fuel; and 11.2 million sets of military uniform.

Three of a set of six training posters of the 1960s depicting the basic infantry skills that every member of the PLA had to master: here, throwing grenades, use of satchel charges, and digging-in. The others covered shooting, bayonet-fighting, and swimming with personal weapons and equipment. Note that at this date none of the soldiers is shown wearing a helmet. (*China* Magazine)

Other theaters and events:

1962 In October–November, India and China fought a brief border skirmish that resulted in a Chinese military victory. The clash was initiated when India granted asylum to the 14th Dalai Lama, and began to place a number of outposts north of the McMahon Line on what the Chinese regarded as Chinese territory.

1967–76 China entered a long period of internal chaos; during this **Cultural Revolution** political infighting would hinder economic, social and military development. The PLA's operations during this period must be seen against that background.

The 1969 Sino-Soviet border skirmishes

Although disputed ownership of Zhēnbǎo (Damanskii) Island in the Ussuri River was a hangover from the days of Imperial China and Tsarist Russia, during the era of communist solidarity frontier patrols of each nation often exchanged greetings, and the disputed border line was never a problem. However, during the Cultural Revolution increasing Sino-Soviet tensions led to brawls between patrols, and shooting broke out in March 1969. The USSR responded with tanks and APCs as well as artillery bombardment. Over three days the PLA successfully halted Soviet penetration and eventually evicted all Soviet troops from the island. During this skirmish the PLA deployed two reinforced infantry platoons from 3rd Co, 202nd Regt of 68th

During the Zhēnbǎo Island clashes with the Soviet Army in March 1969 one Chinese RPG team, Huá Yùjié (left) and his assistant Yú Hǎicháng, destroyed four AFVs and achieved more than 10 kills. Huá and Yú received the accolade "Combat Hero" from the CMC, and their action was commemorated on a postage stamp. In this posed photo they wear the fleece-flapped cap and padded Model 65 winter uniform. (*China* Magazine)

Div with artillery backup. According to Chinese sources, the Soviet Army initially deployed some 60 soldiers and six BTR-60PBs, and in a second attack some 100 troops backed up by 10 tanks and 14 APCs, as well as artillery including BM-21 "Katyusha" rockets. (In the ensuing battle a Soviet T-62 tank fell through the ice and sank, but was eventually recovered by PLA divers; it is now displayed at the Běijīng Military Museum.) Other notable border incidents in this period included a clash at Tiělièkètí in China's Xīnjiāng Province in August 1969, when a PLA patrol of 22 soldiers and three journalists were surrounded by about 300 Soviet troops with supporting arms, and annihilated.

This incident and the Zhēnbǎo Island skirmishing almost led to all-out war between China and the Soviet Union, with each side massing huge numbers of troops at the border. However, the border disputes were subsequently resolved when China, Russia and Kazakhstan signed agreements to ratify their frontier lines.

Chinese characters of slogan "Service to the People," associated with Máo badges (see Plate B3a).

为人民服务

THE 1960s

(1) Female soldier, Model 65 uniform
The Model 65 uniform was devoid of all insignia except for a large red star cap badge and plain red collar patches. The female soldier's equivalent of the "Máo cap" was peakless, and tended to be worn pushed back on the head; some photos show a line of red piping at the crown seam. Regulations for female soldiers were more relaxed, allowing more variety of hair styles, though simple fringes and/or pigtails were the most common. Before the mid-1990s uniforms did not include any shirt or undergarments, and it was common to see a privately purchased civilian blouse worn under the green jacket. Medical personnel displayed the red Geneva Cross on a loose armband attached with a safety pin.

(2) Soldier in bayonet training
At the height of the Sino-Soviet border disputes the PLA were prepared for invasion by the Soviet Army at any time. Basic bayonet-fighting techniques were taught with dummy rifles, and protective gear in the style of Japanese *kendo* equipment, with stiff leather "armor plates" attached to the front and left side of quilted garments; here it is worn over the padded Model 65 winter uniform.

(3) Cold-weather field uniform, Soviet border
The padded Model 65 winter uniform is worn with an *ushanka* of synthetic fleece, thick mittens, and a snow-camouflage cape. During the Cultural Revolution every citizen was expected to wear a "Máo pin" (see 3a above); the slogan at the base, "Service to the People," is still popular today. His weapon is a Soviet-made SKS semiautomatic rifle, distinguishable by its folding knife bayonet from the Chinese-made Type 56 with a spike bayonet, and his webbing has eight pouches for its magazines. A water canteen is slung to his left hip.

1

3a

2

3

THE 1970s:
The 1979 Sino-Vietnamese War

After the PAVN's 1972 spring offensive against the Army of the Republic of Vietnam failed, China soon made up the tremendous material losses, and in 1975 the North Vietnamese were able to launch the offensive that led to final victory. After the fall of Saigon direct military aid from Běijīng ceased, but Chinese support continued; for example, China established a torpedo-boat building yard, and factories for the production of light and heavy machine guns, AA guns, and ammunition. Although Sino-Vietnamese relations began to sour during the 1970s such aid continued until 1978, just before the Sino-Vietnamese War of the following year. In February 1979 China entered into a month-long war with Vietnam under the pretext of self-defense after numerous Vietnamese incursions into China that had resulted in deaths and damage to civilian property.

The decision for war was taken by the Central Military Commission on December 8, 1978, and preparations were completed by January 8, 1979. The PLA massed a force of 560,000 troops, divided into 9 corps, 29 infantry divisions, 2 artillery divisions and 2 AA divisions, supported by the Railroad, Engineer and Construction corps as well as local militias. The main thrust entered North Vietnam from two directions on February 17, 1979. An attacking force of 100,000 from Yúnnán Province in the west, commanded by Yáng Dézhì, and another 100,000 from Guǎngxī Province in the east, headed by Xǔ Shìyǒu, formed the key spearheads. Facing the Chinese on these fronts were six Vietnamese infantry divisions (3, 316A, 337, 338, 345 & 346), 16 local and 4 artillery regiments, giving a total of 100,000 troops.

Sino-Vietnamese border country, 1984: men of a PLA commando group taking a cigarette break. They wear Model 74 uniforms, and this was the first conflict for which steel helmets were issued. The soldier at left carries a Model 77 stick grenade in his webbing; such wooden-handled grenades are still in PLA use today, being less costly to manufacture than all-metal "egg" grenades. Note the foreground soldier's plain red collar patches; during the Cultural Revolution military ranks were abolished – there were only "soldiers" and "officers." During this period they were often addressed according to their appointment, such as "Comrade Squad Commander" or "Comrade Company Commander." (*China* Magazine)

The principal objective of Xǔ's Guǎngxī command was the capture of Cao Bang by means of a pincer movement, with 41st Corps advancing from the southeast spearheaded by 122nd and 123rd Divs, and 42nd Corps attacking from the northwest with 125th and 126th Divs in the lead. Facing them were local units backed by the PAVN 346 Division. In the first three hours the eastern prong broke through to Thông Nông (in Chinese, Tongnóng), but met heavy resistance at Trà Lĩnh (Cháling). Xǔ's second objective was Lang Son (Liàngshān), protected by the PAVN 3 Division. With 55th and 43rd Corps in the lead, the PLA first annihilated stubborn resistance around an old French fort at Dong Deng (Tóngdēng), then penetrated as far as Mong Cai (Mángjiē), Lộc Bình (Lùpíng), and later Khau Ma (Kòumǎshān). After the encirclement of Lang Son on March 2 the PAVN 308 Div counterattacked, but were beaten back. In the western sector, Yáng's objective was Lào Cai (Lǎojiē), which he attacked with 11th, 13th and 14th Corps. Facing the Chinese on this front were the Vietnamese 316A and 345 Divs, but the town fell by February 22. After achieving its stated objectives, on March 5 the PLA declared a ceasefire and started to withdraw; the last vehicle crossed the frontier at 22.30hrs on March 15.

Despite achieving its strategic objectives and overwhelming stiff Vietnamese resistance, the PLA suffered significant losses. According to Chinese sources this war cost the PLA 6,954 killed and 14,800-plus wounded. Again according to the Chinese, Vietnamese casualties were as high as 80,000. (However, a Vietnamese publication claims that Chinese losses were as high as 20,000 dead and 60,000 wounded, and 280 tanks.) The PLA learned valuable lessons from this brief but hard-fought war. The organizational havoc caused by the Cultural Revolution, with its insistence on a rankless military structure, had created serious confusion and administrative chaos.

THE 1980s:
Renewed Sino-Vietnamese hostilities, 1980 & 1984–91

The ceasefire of 1979 did not bring peace; the Vietnamese artillery continued harassing fire across the border, and a series of small frontier clashes began almost immediately. What may be described as a battle for the border highlands was fought over a series of peaks straddling the Sino-Vietnamese frontier on both the former battle fronts. In 1980 a company-size clash occurred on Luójiāpíng Mountain in Yúnnán Province, and the following year further fighting took place on the 1,705m (5,592ft) Kòulín Mountain, and for Bālǐhé East Hill. In the eastern sector, a more serious battle for Fǎkǎ Mountain in Guǎngxī Province lasted for 57 days in 1980, when soldiers from the Guǎngzhōu Military Region's 2nd Bn, 9th Regt, 3rd Inf Div fought against elements of the PAVN's 52 Regt, 337 Division.

Prolonged and larger-scale combats in the western sector, considered by many as the PLA's second punitive campaign against the PAVN, broke out in April 1984 and lasted until 1991 in the border region of China's Yúnnán Province and Vietnam's Ha Giang (Héjiāng) Province. In 1984 China initiated a series of actions to capture hills astride the frontier; the PLA's furthest incursion was no deeper than 5km (3 miles), but capturing this high ground enabled the Chinese to dominate the surrounding area and push the Vietnamese outside artillery range from the border. To the Chinese this series of actions are known as the battles of Lǎo Shān and Zhěyīn Shān, but in Vietnam they are collectively known as the battle of Yi Xuyen. On April 28,

Still wearing the "Máo cap" of the Model 65 uniform, this soldier in the jungled hills on the North Vietnamese border, photographed in about 1988, has a first-generation camouflage suit in "woodland" pattern. His weapon is the folding-stock Type 56-1 assault rifle. (*China* Magazine)

1984 the 40th Div of the PLA 14th Corps attacked Lǎo Mountain while the 49th Div of 16th Corps headed for Zhěyīn Mountain; the PAVN 313 Div and batteries of 168 Arty Bde conducted a fighting withdrawal.

The contest for these highlands bickered on over many years, with frequent artillery duels, and PLA units were constantly rotated to give commanders combat experience. By 1991 the two nations eventually agreed a border demarcation by which China gained all the disputed territories, thus securing the advantage of the high ground in the frontier zone. However, these hostilities against Vietnam in the 1980s again exposed major deficiencies within the PLA. There was a serious need to invest in quality rather than quantity, and, as part of badly needed reforms, in 1985 the CMC announced a million-man reduction in overall strength.

Consequences of the Tiananmen Square incident, 1989

This controversial internal security operation blighted the reputation of the PLA. Instances of blatant insubordination occurred, loyalties were questioned, and subsequent purges were carried out at many levels of the PLA. One consequence would be a clear separation of national defense and internal security responsibilities between the PLA and the People's Armed Police (PAP).

THE 1990s TO DATE:

1991 saw the PLA's first overseas deployment as part of a United Nations "blue beret" peacekeeping force, to Cambodia, following the final withdrawal of the PAVN occupation forces. Subsequent UN deployments included the Congo and Liberia in 1993. Between 1995 and 2000, further cuts of 500,000 men were made; the PLA Ground Forces avoided most of these, at the expense of the PLA/Navy and PLA/Air Force. In 1997 and 1999 respectively, political agreements brought the peaceful transfer to China of sovereignty over the last vestiges of the old "treaty ports" – Hong Kong from Great Britain, and Macau from Portugal – and the PLA took over the defense of these two Special Administrative Regions.

Lebanon, 2006: PLA officers wearing the pale blue UN beret and cravat with "woodland" camouflage uniforms. On the left is Maj Li. Shaking hands with the UN Secretary General is Col Luo, who displays a round UN patch on his right sleeve. Note rank insignia worn on shoulder straps. Both officers wear woven English-language name and "China Army" tags above their right and left breast pockets.

In the first decade of the 21st century, the PLA made further UN deployments to Sudan in 2005 and the following year to Lebanon. In 2008 China was hit by two great natural disasters. The snowstorms in January, and the 8.0 Richter-scale earthquake in Sichuan later that year, tested the ability of the modern PAP and PLA to mount civil aid missions in all quarters, especially in the areas of logistics, medical aid and mobilization.

PLA standard guard of the Hong Kong Garrison at the National Day parade in October 2011. They wear Model 07 honor guard uniforms for (left to right) the PLA Navy, PLA Ground Forces and PLA Air Force. To be selected, all members must be over 6 feet tall; as the senior service the Army always provides the standard-bearer and the other services the guards, here armed with QBZ-95 assault rifles. The soldier's honor guard distinctions, introduced with the Model 87 uniform, include golden-yellow aiguillettes on his left shoulder, three diagonal stripes on his cuffs, and double-striped trousers tapered into cavalry-style boots. (Author's photo)

THE PLA TODAY

The PLA is not a purely military organization, but the principal instrument of the state – an indispensable institution that has played central roles in the development of the People's Republic of China. For example, in the early years of the republic there were no standardized national police or firefighting services, and the PLA often had to step in to perform these essential tasks. Surplus PLA soldiers or whole units were assigned to different duties as and when the state demanded. Later these transfers were made permanent, with such PLA personnel being "rebadged" as police, firefighters, border guards, judges, etc.

Once a part of the PLA but since disbanded, the PLA Railroad Corps (Zhōngguó Rénmín Jiěfàngjūn Tiědàobīng) not only contributed to the wars in Korea and Vietnam, but played an important part in the development of China from 1950 to 1984. It built thousands of bridges, tunnels, and roads as well as more than 965,000km (600,000 miles) of railroad tracks. In 1984 the corps was absorbed into the Railroad Ministry, but under the 1990s reforms these departments were privatized; some became very profitable, and were listed on the stockmarket. (For example, the former 2nd Div of the PLA Railroad Corps, with an illustrious history in the Chinese Civil War, Korean War and Sino-Vietnamese War, became in 1984 the 12th Engineering Dept

Chinese characters "Shanghai Militia" (see Plate C4).

C **THE 1970s–1980s**

(1) Infantry soldier, North Vietnam border fighting, c.1984
This infantryman wears the FK-80 steel helmet – not available during the 1979 war – and the Model 65 uniform, with puttees. He is armed with a 7.62mm Type 56 assault rifle, the Chinese version of the Soviet AK-47. His chest webbing has three long magazine pouches on the front and two shorter pouches for grenades on each side. In one of the latter he carries a stick grenade; another common item was a separate slung canvas carrier for four of these. On his right hip he has a utility haversack for small kit. The canvas-topped, rubber-soled footwear were known as "liberation shoes."

(2) PLA reversible camouflage uniform; North Vietnam border fighting, c.1984
This soldier, on operations in the forested mountains of the border country between China's Yúnnán Province and Vietnam's Ha Giang Province, holds a Chinese-made Type 56-1 folding-stock assault rifle. The very first PLA camouflage clothing, reportedly used by some elite troops from the mid-1970s, was in a "DPM"-type pattern of two shades of green, brown, and black. It was soon followed by this first-generation reversible uniform, worn from the late 1970s into the mid-1980s; the "duck hunter" pattern was on the inside, reversing to a "woodland" pattern. Other slight color variations on this reversible uniform have been illustrated.

(2a) "Woodland" pattern, c.1984
The pattern on the outside of the reversible unform; all pockets were on this side.

(3) Honor Guard, winter dress uniform, 1972
This fine-looking soldier, picked for his height of at least 6 feet, is one of the honor guard drawn up at Nanyuan Airport in February 1972 to greet US President Richard Nixon arriving for his historic visit to China. The Model 65 uniform still bears only a plain red cap star and collar patches. It is worn with an *ushanka*-style hat with flaps of dark brown artificial fur, a double-breasted greatcoat with a collar of the same pile material, and white cotton gloves. His brown leather belt has a silver frame-and-plate buckle, and supports a single old-fashioned box-type ammunition pouch. The weapon is the Type 56 semiautomatic rifle.

(4) Shanghai Militia, 1970s
In stark contrast to the appearance of the previous figure, this young woman nevertheless carries the same weapon, and has been issued with a set of waist webbing (though its pockets seem to be empty). She wears her own clothing – a white blouse, dark blue bib-front factory dungarees, and traditional lightweight black fabric shoes. The label in the clear plastic cover pinned to the bib reads "Shanghai Militia" in black inside a red frame. Like all Chinese citizens during the era of the Cultural Revolution, she wears one of the almost obligatory Máo badges.

In the early days of the People's Republic about 175,000 PLA personnel were transferred to a civil development role in order to open up large areas of the Western desert region for cultivation and settlement. This Xīnjiāng Production & Construction Corps was responsible for a wide variety of tasks including building, agriculture, forestry work and desert-reclamation programs. This photo was taken in the early 1960s, when the work was still being carried out mainly with muscle-power, picks and shovels.

of the Railroad Ministry, based in the city of Taiyuan in Shanxi Province of Northern China; eventually privatized in 1998, it became the commercial 12th Railroad Engineering Group.) Such origins in the PLA are shared by many of the largest corporations in China, in fields from mining and construction to pharmaceuticals and the manufacture of consumer goods.

Another unique institution is the Xinjiang Production & Construction Corps (Xīnjiāng Shēngchǎn Jiànshè Bīngtuán). Technically nowadays not part of the PLA, it is a socio-economic paramilitary organization with a unique role to "develop and protect Xinjiang Uygur Autonomous Region." Today it has a workforce of close to a million, organized into 14 divisions, 174 regimental farms and 5,000 companies, with a sizable militia capacity. The organization is now a private entity, known officially as the China Xinjiang Development Group Company, but to the majority of Chinese it is still known affectionately as "the Corps" (Bīngtuán).

The Infrastructure Engineering Corps (Jiěfàngjūn Jīběn Jiànshè Gōngchéngbing), also once a part of the PLA, was tasked with protecting the nation's gold and other mineral assets, hydroelectric power, reservoirs and water resources. These duties are now part of the remit of the People's Armed Police. In the 1970s–80s, to supplement meager incomes and unit funds, the PLA was encouraged to operate businesses, mostly farms and food services but later diversifying into hotels, taxi services, and others. A few members of the military got very rich as a result, and greed, corruption, and illegal activities marred combat effectiveness; in 1988 the PLA was ordered to divest itself of purely commercial involvements except for some strategically important enterprises.

ORGANIZATION

The Chinese armed forces are the key element in the overall Chinese security apparatus, alongside the civilian police (under the Ministry of Public Security, MPS), and the Bureau of National Security, in charge of domestic and international intelligence-gathering (under the Ministry of State Security, MSS). The MPS and MSS are civilian organizations reporting to the State Council headed by the Prime Minister. The Chinese armed forces are responsible to the Central Military Commission, headed by its all-powerful Chairman, who under normal circumstances is the President of the People's Republic of China.

Regular forces

The armed forces consist of the PLA and its sub-services, the People's Armed Police, and the Militia. The PLA is responsible for countering external threats; the PAP's primary role is internal security, with a secondary role of supporting the PLA in times of national crisis. The Militia also has the primary duty of external defense, but assists in maintaining domestic security if the situation demands. The PAP and Militia also report to the State Council, especially in domestic matters, since they work in conjunction with the civilian police.

Gen Liáng Guānglè (b.1940), the Minister for National Defense at the time of writing, and a former Chief of the General Staff (2002–07). General Liáng currently serves as a State Councillor and a member of the Central Military Commission. He is seen here wearing Model 87 uniform with a PLA Ground Forces badge on the standing collar of his dress tunic, and his rank displayed on the Soviet-style shoulder boards – three stars above a wreath, in gold metal, on gold lace boards edged in red. (US Dept of Defense; photo Staff Sgt D. Myles Cullen, USAF)

The PLA includes the Army (in this text, for clarity, termed the Ground Forces), the PLA Navy (PLA/N), PLA Air Force (PLA/AF), and the strategic missile force (Second Artillery Corps, SAC), with Reserve units for each element. The total size of the PLA is some 2.3 million: about 1.6 million in the Ground Forces, 255,000 in the PLA/N and 400,000 in the PLA/AF, with 100,000 in the SAC. Reserve forces are estimated at about 800,000 strong. Special forces were added to each of the three armed services from the early 1990s, as were new high-technology units such as electronic and cyber warfare, information warfare, and psychological warfare elements.

The Ground Forces are divided between a main force usually known as the Field Army, which is dispersed throughout the country, and specifically-tasked local forces, such as coastal defense and frontier guard units. The Ground Forces are organized into combined-arms formations known as "group armies;" the closest Western equivalent to this Chinese term (Jítuán Jūn) is the army corps. The other main PLA command echelons are the division (Shī), brigade (Lǚ), regiment (Tuán), battalion (Yíng), company (Lián), platoon (Pái), and section (Bān).

Reserve forces

Before the establishment of the PLA Reserve component in 1983 there were only regular forces and militia. Like the Territorial Army in the UK or the National Guard in the USA, the PLA Reserve components are essentially civilians in uniform. Many are technical specialists, e.g. medical or electronic

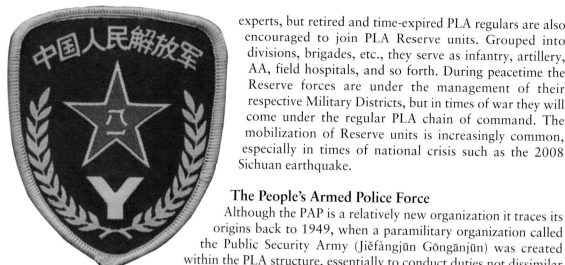

experts, but retired and time-expired PLA regulars are also encouraged to join PLA Reserve units. Grouped into divisions, brigades, etc., they serve as infantry, artillery, AA, field hospitals, and so forth. During peacetime the Reserve forces are under the management of their respective Military Districts, but in times of war they will come under the regular PLA chain of command. The mobilization of Reserve units is increasingly common, especially in times of national crisis such as the 2008 Sichuan earthquake.

The People's Armed Police Force

Although the PAP is a relatively new organization it traces its origins back to 1949, when a paramilitary organization called the Public Security Army (Jiěfàngjūn Gōngānjūn) was created within the PLA structure, essentially to conduct duties not dissimilar from those of today's PAP. Many subsequent twists and turns reflected a continuing indecision about whether this entity was to be part of the Police or Army. This led to repeated and confusing changes of title: to Chinese PLA Internal Guard Troops (Zhōngguó Rénmín Jiěfàngjūn Nèiwèi Bùduì); People's Public Security Troops (Rénmín Wǔzhuāng Bùduì); PLA Public Security Troops (Zhōngguó Rénmín Jiěfàngjūn Gōngān Bùduì);16th Dept, Ministry of Public Security & Associated Armed Police (Gōngānbù 16jú Jí Suǒshǔ Wǔzhuāng Jǐngchá); and PLA General Staff Department Garrison Unit & Associated Public Security Troops (Jiěfàngjūn Zǒngcān Jǐngbèibù Jí Suǒshǔ Gōngān Bùduì). These finally culminated in 1983 in the Chinese People's Armed Police Force (Zhōngguó Rénmín Wǔzhuāng Jǐngchá Bùduì).

Shoulder sleeve patch of a PLA Reserve unit, Model 07 uniform. The script across the top, as on all Ground Forces patches, reads Zhōngguó Rénmín Jiěfàngjūn, "China People's Liberation Army." The red star bears the characters "8.1" recalling the PLA's foundation date, and the letter "Y" is the abbreviation for Yùbèi, "Reserve." (Author's photo)

D THE 1980s

(1) Female medical officer, Model 87 uniform
Representing the widespread reforms of the later 1980s, this lieutenant wears the Model 87 uniform, with a deep Red Cross armband. The officer's peaked cap, with red band and piping and silver chin cords, is unchanged from the intermediate Model 85 uniform. However, the 1987 badge differs from the 1985 design at the base; it now has two sprays of leaves and a palace motif above a reversed arc of crenellations, in place of the Model 85's upright crenellations superimposed on the bottom of the circular wreath. The collar badges are red stars with the "8.1" characters, set with the points in the intervals of a pentogram of gold rays **(see 6)**. Her two silver rank stars are displayed on gold braid shoulder boards with red edges and center stripe. The belt has a silver buckle plate embossed with the star and "8.1;" it supports a holstered Model 54 pistol (the Chinese copy of the Soviet TT-33).

(2) *Artiste*, PLA Ground Forces entertainment troupe
The PLA follows the Soviet example, incorporating entertainment troupes within the army itself. Their members are highly qualified, and today many go on to enjoy careers as movie stars and best-selling recording artists. At this date they wore a more attractively tailored version of the Model 87 uniform, buttoning right-over-left in female style, with their own distinctions: collar patches with a star-and-leaves motif, special shoulder boards, and gold aiguillettes on

the right shoulder. There are no rank structures in the PLA entertainment troupes, but they obey military regulations and undergo rudimentary military training.

Model 85 and Model 87 insignia:
(3) Model 87 uniform shoulder board, entertainment troupe. The red background identified the Army; black and royal blue versions were worn in the PLA/N and PLA/AF troupes respectively.
(4) Model 87 uniform chest pin, Administration officer. The Chinese characters spell "Administrative Position," and are picked out in the color of the service – again, red denotes the Ground Forces.
(5) Model 85 uniform officer's collar patch. The intermediate style, between the minimalism of the Cultural Revolution and the full reintroduction of ranks; the unpiped edge of the patch butts against the edge of the collar. Enlisted ranks' patches lacked the yellow piping, but all ranks wore a single star pin.
(6) Model 85 uniform Reserve soldier's collar patch. Note the "Y" on the red star, for "Yubei" = Reserve.
(7) Model 87 uniform, working dress shoulder strap, Reserve 2nd lieutenant. Rank insignia have reappeared at last, here on a type of dark olive-green shoulder strap that had a "velvet" appearance. Again, the "Y" stands for "Yubei".
(8) Model 87 uniform, working dress shoulder strap, Militia 2nd lieutenant. "M" denotes "Min Bing" = Militia.

The original forerunner of today's People's Armed Police was the PLA Public Security Army (Jiěfàngjūn Gōngānjūn), formed in 1949. These troops are armed with leftover Japanese Arisaka Type 38 rifles. The left arm badge bears the Chinese character for "Gōngān" and a red star.

Formed from former PLA border guard and internal security units as well as some elements of the Police, the PAP is currently about 1.5 million strong, organized into contingents for each province and city. These perform a variety of tasks ranging from border and forest security, firefighting, the security of hydroelectric power supplies and gold mines, to providing VIP protection and anti-terrorist SWAT teams, and sometimes road construction and the transportation of specialized goods. The PAP wear different uniforms from the PLA but often in the same drab green shade, and their similar rank structure to the PLA confuses many onlookers. Although recruits for the PLA and PAP are gathered at the same induction periods, and the PAP is subject to PLA regulations, the PAP has its own training institutions separate from the PLA.

The PAP's latest armored personnel carrier, known as the Type 08, seen here at the 2009 National Day parade. It is armed with twin-barrel water cannon and a 7.62mm GPMG.

A poster drawn by Féng Yǒukāng in August 1975, depicting a somewhat idealized image of Militia Unit 6386 of the PLA Shanghai garrison command. Militia units of the 1970s were mostly responsible for local defense duties such as coastal and AA artillery, frontier patrols, etc.; they were issued some equipment but not uniforms, and wore civilian clothing. (IISH/Stefan R. Landsberger Collections)

The Militia

Militia units have played a key role in supporting the PLA in many of the epic battles of its history, from the Civil War in the 1940s to the Sino-Vietnamese clashes of the 1980s. Since 1987 the Militia has been upgraded to two categories, the "primary" and "ordinary" militia. The former is organized into QRF for local emergences, from national security to natural disaster relief. Women are eligible for enlistment in the primary militia, but they have mostly served in the ordinary militia.

According to the 2004 Defense Plan, the primary militia is 10 million strong. Since all male citizens from 18 to 35 years of age not already serving in the armed services are technically liable for militia service, this theoretically means almost everybody. In practice, enlistment is very selective and only a small proportion of the population are active members. Militia units from regiment down to squad level exist in almost every city, district, county, and village, as well as in state-owned enterprises and factories. The annual commitment is a minimum of 30 days for officers and SNCOs and 15 days for the rank-and-file. While some units are effective organizations, others exist simply on paper, and the actual training conducted is highly questionable. Currently the Militia is being streamlined, with an emphasis on quality rather than quantity. The Militia assists the PLA by performing security and logistic functions in wartime, including AA, communications, chemical defense, engineering, and the repair of infrastructure. Recently private citizens with special skills such as languages and computer technology have been roped into urban militias to provide support for the PLA or the PAP in maintaining public security.

COMMAND STRUCTURE

The Central Military Commission – all of whom must be CCP members – exercise the supreme control over the PLA. The following report directly to the CMC: the four General Headquarters Departments; the three senior military academies; the seven Military Regions, and the garrisons of the two Special Administrative Regions (Hong Kong and Macau); and the People's Armed Police (who also report to the State Council).

General Headquarters Departments

The CMC sets policies and directives, which are executed by the four General Headquarters Departments. The General Staff Department (GSD, Zǒng Cānmóubù) is responsible for operations, intelligence, electronic warfare, communications, military affairs, training, mobilization, meteorological, survey and cartographic functions, and foreign affairs.

The General Political Department (GPD, Zǒng Zhèngzhìbù) is responsible for the political and ideological reliability and training of the PLA, including morale, public relations and publicity (e.g. dance troupes, museums, media, and sports). Most importantly, the GPD is responsible for personnel matters, Party discipline, internal security, legal affairs, the maintaining of dossiers, and promotions. The GPD controls officers known as political commissars (Zhèng Wěi) at battalion and higher levels, and political instructors (Zhǐdǎo Yuán) at company level and below, in both PLA and PAP units. At all levels of the PLA, principal commanders (or primary staff officers) and their respective political officers usually share the same rank, just as they share responsibility for the performance of their units. Through this system the CCP ensures the absolute loyalty of the PLA to the Party; as Máo Zédōng stated, "The Party commands the gun, and the gun must never be allowed to command the Party." The political commissar is a uniformed military officer, representing the CCP as the head of a Party cell within the unit. While largely responsible for administrative tasks such as public relations and counseling, he sometimes serves as second-in-command.

At the time of writing, Gen Guō Bóxióng (b.1942) is the Vice Chairman of the CMC. Here he is seen during a visit to the USA, wearing the waist-length summer shirt order of Model 07 uniform, with the shoulder slides of his rank, and a plastic name tag incorporating the national flag. (US Dept of Defense; photo L/Cpl Kelly R Chase, USMC)

The General Logistic Department (GLD, Zǒnghòu Qínbù) is responsible for finances and auditing, military supplies to all branches of the PLA, health services, transportation, barracks and other military infrastructure. It also supervises factories and farms operated by the PLA. (The PLA produces much of its own food, from livestock to grains, vegetables and fruit, in order to supplement unit mess funds).

The General Armament Department (GAD, Zǒng Zhuāngbèibù) is responsible for the weapons and equipment of the PLA. It conducts maintenance and repairs as well as research and development, including the procurement of major weapons, equipment, and ammunition.

Senior-level military academies

Three of these institutions report to the CMC. The Academy of Military Science (AMS, Jūnshì Kēxuéyuàn) is primarily a research center for military strategy, operations and tactics, military systems, military history, and foreign militaries. The National Defense University (NDU, Guófáng Dàxué) provides courses to senior and staff officers of the PLA and PAP, civilian researchers and senior civil servants. These include the three-month National

The Seven Military Regions
七大军区

Map of China showing the seven Military Regions. The Macau SAR is immediately west of the Hong Kong SAR. In case of hostilities a war zone with a separate HQ would be formed; this would not necessarily correspond with the boundaries of existing MRs, and would vary according to operational needs. (Author's map)

Defense Course for officers awaiting promotion, and refresher courses for officers assigned to new posts. The students of the National University of Defense Technology (NUDT, Guófáng Kējì Jìshú Dàxué) are senior scientists and engineers, commanders of technical units or military-run scientific and technical research institutes, and cadets who will enter the PLA to serve in technical branches.

Military Regions and local commands

The Republic is divided into seven Military Regions (MR, Jūnqū), each named after the city where its HQ is located: Shěnyáng, Běijīng, Lánzhōu, Jǐnán, Nánjīng, Guǎngzhōu, and Chéngdū. There are also two Special Administrative Regions – Hong Kong and Macau - on the coast of Guǎngzhōu MR. Under each MR are several Military Districts (MD) and key city garrisons. Each MR contains units of the three armed services that can be formed into a "group army," or independent divisions, brigades, etc. Each MR commander is supported by several deputies, as well as a political commissar and his deputies. A chief-of-staff oversees representatives from the four General Headquarters Departments and other staff officers.

Each Military District is responsible for a single province, and bears its province's or region's name. Like those of the Military Regions, MD commanders are responsible for the local and reserve forces in their province and for mobilization preparations, and coordinate closely with local government and PAP forces. The latter perform duties similar to the military police of Western armies, ranging from guarding military facilities to supervising troops when they are away from barracks. Under each MD are a number of Military Sub-Districts (MSD). Essentially a miniature MD, the MSD also plays an essential role in organizing annual conscription (see under "Personnel," below).

PLA rifleman in Model 87 "woodland" camouflage combat dress and QGF-03 helmet. (The first Chinese "Fritz" helmet was the experimental FK-96, a steel copy of the US PASGT, but a similar QGF-02 made in a ballistic composite material was seen at the time of the handover of Hong Kong in 1997). For this ceremonial occasion a woven PLA cap badge is displayed on his helmet cover, and in addition to the official shoulder rank slide he has a Ground Forces honor guard badge loosely attached to his sleeve. He is armed with the 5.8mm QBZ-95 assault rifle, and wears Type 91 PCG. (US Dept of Defense; photo Gunnery Sgt Demetrio J. Espinosa, USMC)

CURRENT TACTICAL ORGANIZATION

Successive military reforms in the PLA have been an almost continuous process. In 1949 the PLA was largely a mass infantry army with 70-plus "army"-size formations (equivalent to a Western army corps); today the PLA Ground Forces comprise just 18 all-arms "group armies." Prior to 1985, before the establishment of the "group army," the PLA was organized on a standard Soviet triangular model – i.e. three regiments formed a division, three divisions an army, etc. – and there was a strict demarcation between the arms of service. Nowadays the PLA follows a totally all-arms concept, allowing the independent maneuvering of all-arms strike forces tailored to the threat, the task, and the geographical area.

Unit identification

PLA and PAP units are identified by a multitude of names. Besides the standard unit and formation designators (e.g. 38th Armored Division), all PLA and PAP units – including institutes, academies, and military factories – are also identified by a special five-digit numerical code (e.g. 65521 Unit). This practice is common in communist countries, as a means of confusing foreign intelligence-gatherers as to the true nature of the unit or organization. Some units have also been given honorific titles commemorating past accomplishments – e.g., "The Good Company of the Nanjing Road," and "The Bayonet-Point Hero Company." In recent years some units have created their own unit patches, but the PLA tends to avoid distinctive unit insignia for security reasons.

Squad to battalion

The PLA infantry battalion is made up of similar building blocks to any Western army, in sections/squads, platoons, and companies. The PLA rifle squad is 9–12 strong, depending on task and organization, and the standard 9-man squad is composed as follows:

Role	Rank	Weapon
Gunner	Private	Type 81 LMG/ or QBB-95 LSW
Assistant gunner	Private	Type 81/QBZ-95 rifle
Anti-tank gunner	Private	Type 69 140mm RPG/PF-98 120mm
Assistant gunner	Private	Type 81/QBZ-95 rifle
Squad leader	JNCO	Type 81/QBZ-95 rifle
Riflemen x3	Privates	Type 81/QBZ-95 rifles
Sniper	Private	Type 85 (improved Dragunov SVD) or QBU-88 marksman's rifle

However, in mechanized units the squad is organized into two 5-man fire teams headed by the squad leader and an assistant squad leader (usually a JNCO), each with an LSW and a grenadier as well as 2 riflemen; each fire-team leader is equipped with a small radio. The squad's riflemen carry the latest 5.8mm QBZ-95 assault rifle (QBZ = "Light Infantry Weapon, Rifle,

Automatic") and 500 rounds of ammunition (300 rounds for the rifleman, 200 for the LSW gunner), a multipurpose bayonet, and six WY-91 grenades. The grenadier's QBZ-95 is fitted with an underslung 35mm grenade launcher; he is expected to carry 300 rounds of 5.8mm ammo, 15x 35mm grenade rounds and 2x WY-91 hand grenades. The LSW gunner is equipped with the QBB-95 LSW (QBB = "Light Infantry Weapon, Rifle, Squad use") with 745 rounds of ammunition; the ammo is carried in 3x 75-round drum magazines, 4x 30-round box magazines, and 400 rounds in bandoliers (the fire team's three riflemen contribute another 600 rounds for the LSW – see above). In addition, the LSW gunner has his bayonet and two grenades.

A motor rifles squad dismounted and advancing on the objective, covered by fire from their ZSL-92 6x6 infantry fighting vehicle. Under magnification the soldiers can be seen to wear "woodland" camouflage dress and canvas-and-rubber "liberation shoes" (still popular today), and a mixture of old-style non-integrated load-carrying equipment and Type 01 PCG. The level of equipment in the PLA depends largely upon the readiness category of a particular unit.

The infantry squad's QBB-95 Light Support Weapon, fitted with a drum magazine for 75 rounds of 5.8x42mm ammunition. Each gunner and his assistant carry 745 rounds in magazines and bandoliers, and the other men in the squad carry another 200 rounds each for the LSW. (Author's photo)

The PLA infantry company consists of 8 officers and 184 enlisted ranks divided between the company headquarters, three rifle platoons and one support-weapon platoon. The rifle platoon headquarters comprises a platoon leader (usually a subaltern) and his radio operator, each of them armed with a shortened QBZ-95 assault rifle (609mm instead of 745mm), 300 rounds, bayonet, grenades, and binoculars.

The support-weapon platoon has a 2-man headquarters and four squads. The first squad is equipped with 2x QJZ-89 12.7mm heavy machine guns (some may have the QJZ-77 or -85), each with 800 rounds. Each gun is served by a squad leader or assistant squad leader in command, a gunner, assistant gunner, and armorer/rifleman with QBZ-95 for close protection. It was reported in 2002 that some units have an additional fire-support platoon with the Type 75 14.7mm AA HMG or the newer Type 02. The support platoon also has two light mortar squads, each of 10 men serving 2x PP-93 60mm tubes with 120 rounds (some units may have the QLZ-87 35mm AGL instead), each mortar served by a crew of 4 with a rifleman for close protection. Finally there is an AT missile squad with 2x HJ-9 (Hóngjiàn – "Red Arrow") missile launchers each with 12 rounds, split into two 4-man crews with a rifleman for protection (alternatively, some may have PF-98 120mm AT rockets).

The PLA infantry company HQ has 4 officers and 18 enlisted ranks. The company commander, usually a captain, has a deputy, a political instructor, and a supply/logistics officer or SNCO (Sīwù Zhǎng) in charge of all

E **THE 1990s**

(1) Infantry junior NCO, Model 97 uniform; Hong Kong, July 1, 1997
This Grade 1 JNCO stands to attention as the PLA marches into Hong Kong to take formal possession from Great Britain. He wears a dress version of the Model 97 uniform, with trousers tapered to tuck into black cavalry-style boots. Introduced for the new Hong Kong Garrison, the Model 97 was supposed to become general issue, but in practice it never did, being worn only by the Hong Kong and Macau garrisons. Instead, the Model 87 uniform would have a mid-life extension from October 1, 1999, with small changes made that year, in 2004 and in 2005 taking it through until the general introduction of the Model 07 uniform. Between 1988 and 1999 there had already been a number of revisions to the exact design of the shoulder rank insignia.
Note the new Model 97 cap badge (see 1a). His rank of Grade 1 NCO is identified by one narrow silver chevron on the modified second-generation Model 87 shoulder boards (see 1b). Note also the gold Ground Forces collar badges, of a star set on a wreath over an arc of wall with a central tower. Hidden by his equipment is the pin-on Model 97 Ground Forces right chest badge (see 2a). Temporarily attached to his right sleeve is the Model 97 Hong Kong Garrison patch (see page 54). Over his parade uniform the corporal wears Type 95 Personal Combat Gear i (see 3), and he holds the "bullpup" 5.8mm QBZ-95 assault rifle.

(2) Female senior NCO, Military Police, Hong Kong Garrison
This Grade 5 SNCO wears Model 97 uniform in summer shirtsleeve order, with white cotton gloves and a white plastic "Sam Browne" belt with a gold buckle plate. She owes her rather Western silhouette to her US-style white carbon fiber helmet; this bears a Model 97 cap badge, set on stripes of red over black over royal blue for the PLA's three services, broken each side by the black letters "MP" (English is widely spoken in Hong Kong). Her necktie echoes the red of her shoulder boards of rank (see 2b), which are unique to the Military Police (Xiànbīng). Like E1, she displays the Army's Model 97 right chest pin (see 2a), and also the first, 1997-pattern shoulder patch of the Hong Kong Garrison. PLA personnel in Hong Kong are only allowed to leave their barracks in supervised groups, so – unlike their Western counterparts – MPs do not have to be ready to quell drunken and disorderly soldiers.

(3) Type 95 Personal Combat Gear
This load-carrying equipment was issued to high-profile units, such as the Hong Kong Garrison, which were armed with the QBZ-95 rifle. Made of nylon finished in a woodland camouflage pattern, it does not incorporate a backpack, and soldiers issued with it still have to use the Type 91 or 01 pack. It includes pouches for four rifle magazines, and for four grenades (either the egg-shaped Type 82, 82-1, 82-2 or 82-3, or the older Type 67 or 77 stick grenades – note Velcro loops above pockets to secure stick-grenade handles). At belt level it has (from left to right) a gas mask carrier, a rifle 'scope pouch, a canteen carrier, and the multipurpose bayonet. Not shown here are the additional first aid and utility pouches. The Type 95 PCG was soon replaced with the Type 01 – essentially similar, but made of better rip-stop materials.

1

1a

2

2b

1b

2a

3

China's latest tracked IFV, the ZBD-04, seen taking part in a 2009 National Day parade. This infantry fighting vehicle is armed with one 100mm and one 30mm gun, and three 7.62mm machine guns. It is currently being issued to the two amphibious mechanized divisions in Guǎngzhōu Military Region.

administration. The company HQ also has 2 each radio operators and medics; 6 snipers (more properly, "designated marksmen") equipped with 5.8mm QBU-88 rifles, and a squad of cooks led by an NCO. All except the snipers are equipped with QBZ-95 shortened assault rifles. In technical or mechanized units the company HQ will have additional technical support personnel.

The normal PLA infantry battalion has an HQ, three rifle companies, a mortar company, an antitank company, a reconnaissance platoon, and a medical platoon, for a total of 45 officers and 625 enlisted ranks. In the HQ the battalion commander is normally a major, backed by his deputy, a political officer and supply officers. There are 3 radio operators, 2 admin clerks, 7 security guards and a section of cooks, for a total of 5 officers and 20 enlisted ranks.

The mortar company consists of an HQ and three platoons. Each platoon has an officer commander with a radio operator, and 20 soldiers with 2x PP-87 82mm mortars each with 90 rounds. The company is commanded by a captain, assisted by his deputy, a political officer and a supply officer, 2 radio operators, 4 technical NCOs, and a half-squad of cooks. The AT company also has three platoons, each with 4x HJ-9 ATGM launchers and 72 rounds (though some Class B units – see "Readiness classifications," below – may still be equipped with recoilless rifles). The recon platoon has 1 officer and 21 men, the medical platoon normally 3 doctors and 17 medics. As the situation dictates an antiaircraft platoon may be added, consisting of 1 officer and 28 men equipped with 12x QW-1 or -2 (QW = "Vanguard") shoulder-launched AA missiles, reputedly based on the Russian SA-6 and US Stinger missiles.

Regiment and above

Regiments and brigades are the important level at which true combined-arms organization appears. Since 1998 there has been little difference between the two, and the terms "regiment" and "brigade" are often used interchangeably. The brigade level has become more prominent in the PLA since many divisions have been reduced in size and new brigades formed; the brigade is normally a senior colonel's command. The PLA motorized infantry ("motor rifles") brigade is some 4,500–5,000 strong, consisting of three or sometimes four motorized infantry battalions (the latter mostly in the northern Military Regions, facing the Russians), an artillery regiment, a tank battalion, an engineer battalion, and strong supporting elements.

Each MI battalion has three motor rifles companies and one fire-support company, and is equipped with about 30x ZSL-92 6x6 APCs. This carrier is being upgraded, and some units are now equipped with the ZBL-09 8x8 IFV. Fully mechanized units will be equipped with either the Type 85 (improved Type 63 APC); Type 89 (improved Type 85 with HMG turret); or Type 86 IFV (a copy of the BMP-1). Units in the Nánjīng and Guǎngzhōu MRs were the first to receive the ZBD-04 IFV, unveiled to the public in the 60th National Day parades of October 2009 (see photo opposite).

The tank battalion has 32 tanks; companies normally have a 2-tank HQ and three 4-tank platoons, giving 14 tanks per company. Tanks vary from the antiquated Type 59 to the latest Type 98 and Type 99 MBTs. Two dedicated amphibious divisions (Unit 73021 – the 1st Amphibious MI Div of 1st Group Army, Nánjīng MR; and Unit 75210 – 124th Amphibious MI Div of 42nd Group Army, Guǎngzhōu MR) have the ZTS-63A amphibious tank, an upgraded Type 63 based on the Soviet PT-76. In areas of lesser threats, e.g. Southern China, older tank types such as the Type 62 and Type 63 may still be used.

The artillery's radar, survey, and communications functions are attached to the regimental HQ. The regiment consists of a field artillery battalion, a rocket launcher battalion, and an AA battalion. The field battalion's 18 guns may be either the latest Type 86 or older Type 83 122mm field guns; some units have begun equipping with 152mm howitzers, and these battalions are reduced to company size on account of this increased firepower. The rocket launcher battalion has 18 truck-mounted 130mm Type 82 MBRLs.

Firing the HJ-8E model of the Hóngjiàn ("Red Arrow") ATGM series, a crew-served weapon that can be man-portable or mounted on a jeep. Note the tandem-warhead missile, the guidance wire spooling out, and the back blast. The missile tube ejects to the rear.

Chinese characters: first line, "China People's Liberation Army" – the first two characters read "China," the second two "People's," the last three characters "Liberation Army." Second line, "Macau Garrison" (see Plate F4).

中 国 人 民 解 放 军
驻 澳 门 部 队

第 二 炮 兵

Chinese characters "2nd Artillery" (see Plate F5).

THE PLA IN THE 21st CENTURY

(1) Infantryman, Type 07 digital-pattern camouflage uniform

This PLA soldier of a Class A unit wears the latest "pixelated" camouflage uniform, in the standard "universal" pattern – a neutral pale gray/beige shade, overprinted with a medium grayish-green, medium brown, and small elements in very dark green. His covered helmet is the latest QGF-03. His personal equipment is the latest Type 06 PCG tactical vest, incorporating ballistic armor plates; here it is worn complete with throat and groin protectors. The US-style attachment system of webbing straps allows various layouts of pouches; here it is fitted with four rifle magazine pouches on the front, and (hidden in this pose) a pair of grenade pouches for either egg or stick grenades on each side, and the bayonet. At the level of the integral belt are the bag for a Type 87 respirator (resembling the British S-10) on his right hip, a compass pouch next to it, and a water canteen on the left hip. His main weapon is the 5.8mm folding-stock QBZ-03 assault rifle, and he also carries a Type 54 or 92 semiautomatic pistol in a thigh holster.

(2) Lieutenant Colonel, Chengdu Military Region troops, 2007

This field officer's rank is identified by the two stripes and two stars woven in yellow on his very dark green Model 07 uniform collar patches, which are attached with Velcro. Photographed during a joint exercise with Indian troops, he wears the same digital-pattern camouflage clothing as F1, with a formation patch temporarily attached to his upper right sleeve. Over his combat dress he wears an experimental "Jenkins" load-carrying vest of a type that seems to be unique to the Chengdu MR, in a four-color DPM-type pattern. Note his padded gloves; the pistol in a case on his left ribs balancing the rifle magazine pouches on the right; and the two commercial radios, one at his shoulder and one on his belt.

(2a) Model 07 uniform collar patch, lieutenant colonel

The insignia are yellow for all ranks, and apart from minor differences of detail design they are unchanged from the Model 87 version 2 sequence in use between December 1, 1999 and July 1, 2007. For privates and privates first class they show one and two thin chevrons. For NCO grades the chevrons are surmounted by crossed rifles on a wreath: one thin chevron, one thick, one thin and one thick, and two thick chevrons denote NCOs Grades 1 to 4 respectively (equivalent to ranks from lance corporal to staff sergeant). Crossed rifles on a wreath above one thin and two thick chevrons, and three thick chevrons, identify repectively NCO Grades 4 and 5 (equivalent to warrant officers). Company officers from second lieutenant to captain have one to three stars on a central stripe; field officers from major to senior colonel, one to four stars between two stripes; and brigadier, major and lieutenant generals, one to three stars above an open wreath (a "double spray" of leaves).

(2b) Model 07 uniform collar patch, Administrative officer

The administrative branch has no rank structure as such, just broad officer and NCO categories; this flower-and-ribbon insignia is worn by technical specialists of junior grades, and a flower-and-wreath by more senior grades.

(3) Model 07 uniform service badge

This woven version of the new Ground Forces right breast pin badge has a red stripe and crossed rifles, identifying the Army; General Headquarters staff branches display crossed swords instead. The PLA/N's version features a fouled anchor, and the PLA/AF version wings, each with their own color central stripe.

(4) Model 07 uniform formation patch, Macau Garrison

This shows the typical design and colors of modern formation patches, all with the characters "China People's Liberation Army" in the top line, and the specific title in the second. For instance, the 07 version of the Hong Kong Garrison patch differs from this only in the second line of characters, and in showing the five-petal flower motif at the base in place of this new lotus emblem of the Macau SAR (see page 54). Staff personnel of, for instance, the General Armament Division wear a patch with that title in the second line, and the star, rifles and leafed branches only.

(5) Model 07 uniform formation patch, Second Artillery Corps

The second line of characters reads "Second Artillery;" the rocket motif speaks for itself.

1

2

2b

2a

3

中国人民解放军
驻澳门部队

4

中国人民解放军
第二炮兵

5

Photographed during the 1990s, these troops prepare a defensive position for a 152mm Type 83 self-propelled gun. These SPGs – now judged obsolescent, and in the process of replacement by the PLZ-05 – equipped the three 6-gun batteries of one battalion of the artillery regiment of an armored division. The soldiers wear the FK-80 helmet and "woodland" pattern camouflage uniform, and carry the Type 81 assault rifle.

The mixed AA battalion has four companies. A typical configuration is two companies each equipped with 6x 37mm Type 74 AA guns, one company of PGZ-95 or Type 87 25mm AA guns, and a company with 12x shoulder missile-launchers. The latter are currently either the HY-6 (Hóngyīng = "Red Tassel") or QW-1 or -2 "Vanguard." The brigade also has a strong AT element of company strength. Class A units will have an all-missile unit, but Class B units may still have a mix of AT guns (two platoons of towed 100mm Type 85) and missiles. The missile platoons may have HJ-8 or -9 ATGMs mounted on jeeps, although some may still have the Chinese-made HJ-73C, an improved version of the Soviet AT-3 missile with SACLOS and anti-ERA capability. The modernization program will see the towed 122mm artillery replaced with the 122mm Type 89 SPG, and towed 100mm guns in the AT companies replaced with 6x 100mm PTL-02 6x6 SPATG.

Additional supporting arms for the brigade include a battalion of engineers with flamethrowers, explosives, and mining, construction and bridging capability, as well as means to conduct NBC decontamination for the entire brigade. There is a communications/electronic warfare battalion, and a logistic battalion to maintain all vehicles and arms. Specialist engineering assets unique to the PLA are the 122mm Type 84 truck-mounted, rocket-assisted mine scattering system; the GSL-430 light jeep-mounted mine clearance "hose" charge; the FPH-02 man-portable flamethrower, and the 62mm FHJ-84 twin-barrel, man-portable, reusable incendiary rocket/smoke-screen launcher. Attached to the brigade HQ is an assortment of supporting troops including a recon company, medical team, transportation company, training team, clerks, and radio operators.

The echelon immediately above regiment/brigade is the division, though brigades appear to have become operationally equivalent to divisions now that many former divisions have been downsized into brigades. In the early 1950s, PLA maneuver divisions were organized after the Soviet model: a motorized rifle division had three infantry regiments and a fourth regiment of tanks, and a tank division had three tank regiments and a fourth regiment of motorized infantry. Full-strength PLA infantry and tank divisions followed that structure until the 1990s, when the substitution of the word "armored" (Zhuāngjiǎ) for "tank" (Tǎnkè) division signified the move to the current all-arms configuration.

Readiness classifications

The PLA classifies each formation's state of readiness and strength by letters of the Chinese alphabet – Class A (Jiá) or Class B (Yǐ). The heavier Class A motor rifles divisions are found mostly in the Northern MRs. They are about 18,000 strong, with three five-battalion infantry brigades, a tank regiment, an artillery regiment, and an AA regiment. The Class B division, normally found in Southern China, has only 9,000–10,000 men. It too has three brigades, but each has only four battalions, and each battalion only four companies – three of infantry and a single support company. Some Class B divisions have no attached tank regiment.

The true spearhead of the PLA is the all-arms Class A Group Army, with anything from 50,000 to 70,000 troops, usually commanded by a major general. This formation may have two or three maneuver divisions/brigades, in the latter case either two armored and one motorized infantry formation or vice versa. Some group armies may have air assets such as transport and/ or attack helicopter units attached. The Class B Group Army is 30,000 to 40,000 strong, with one fewer battalions per brigade and one fewer companies per battalion, much weaker fire-support assets, and no attached tank regiments. In addition to its supporting arms assets, each Group Army also has five regimental-size rear echelon units: a training regiment and training depot, military hospital, quartermaster depot, and – uniquely to the PLA – army farms.

Due to sanctions imposed by the West after the 1989 Tiananmen Square incident, China was forced to look again to ex-Soviet sources for much of its military technology, including helicopters. The workhorse of the Army Aviation is the Mi-17; during the great 2008 Wenchun earthquake disaster these locally produced Mi-17s did most of the search-and-rescue work.

The PLA's main scouting and armed helicopter is the Z-9WA, wth an under-nose observation and tracking unit housing low-light TV and infrared search-and-track (IRST), allowing it to operate day or night in all weathers. This helicopter of the Hong Kong Garrison is armed with two 18-round pods of 57mm unguided rockets. (Author's photo)

SOME KEY COMBAT ARMS
Army Aviation

The PLA's Army Aviation Unit (AAU) was formed in January 1988, when it consisted mainly of the PLA/AF's helicopter force transferred to the AAU plus a few Mi-4 helicopters from border patrol units. Reporting directly to the GSD, the AAU is responsible for deploying helicopters and light aircraft to support ground operations, performing antitank, special force insertion, and electronic countermeasure operations. Except for two Y-8 (An-12) transports, all its aircraft are rotary wing. Apart from a small number of special-use machines such as Sikorsky S-70C Black Hawks, Gazelles, and eight Super Pumas for VIP transport, the fleet consists of locally produced types of foreign designs: the Z-8 (Aérospatiale SA 321 Super Frelon), Harbin Z-9 (Eurocopter Dauphin), Z-9W AT gunship (W = Wǔ, "armed") and Mi-17. For training the PLA had been using the Mi-4 and Mi-6 for many years before the advent of the Z-11 (a licensed copy of the French AS-350B Squirrel 7). Chinese sources claim an AAU strength of 500 helicopters, and with the rapid expansion of army aviation each MR is now assigned a helicopter brigade. Each aviation brigade typically controls one to three aviation regiments and supplementary reserve units. There are 10 regular and 9 reserve aviation regiments, plus a training regiment in support.

A PLA tank commander salutes from the cupola of his captured Japanese Type 95 during the first National Day parade in October 1949. (*China* Magazine)

History of an armored division

The following summary of the record of the elite 2nd Armd Div of the 12th Group Army, based in Nánjīng MR, may serve as a microcosm of the experience of the PLA armored force.

In **1949** the East China Armd Regt had 1,460 personnel in two battalions with a total of six companies, equipped with 30x US M3 Stuarts, 10x Japanese Type 97s, and 24x armored cars of various types. (During this period Tank No.102, a Type 97, was awarded the honorary title "Zhū Dé" after the Marshal of the PLA, for its combat performance. It is currently on display at the Military Museum in Běijīng.) Renamed the 1st Armd Regt on July 1, 1949, the unit incorporated a new Amphibious Tank Bn of captured US LVTs. It was subsequently upgraded to divisional status by incorporating 2nd Training Regt of the 24th Army; it then consisted of 1st Armd Regt (3 bns), Amphibious Tank Regt, and a New Armd Regt (2 bns), with a grand total of 149 tanks, 95 miscellaneous armored vehicles, and 162 soft-skin vehicles. The formation was renamed the PLA 2nd Armd Div in **1950**, and the Amphibious Regt received an additional 90x LVTs. In November 1950 the divisional ORBAT showed a Div HQ, 3rd & 4th Tank Regts, 258th Mot Inf Regt, and 306th Mobile Artillery Regiment.

During the **Korean War** two Soviet tank regiments transferred their equipment to the division; by this means the 3rd and 4th Tank Regts each received 30x T-34, 6x JS-2, 4x JSU-122 SPG, and 2x T-34 ARV. The Mobile Arty Regt received one battalion of 12x JSU-122 SPG and two battalions each of 12x 76mm field guns. The 2nd Armd Div was soon deployed to Korea, where it was dispersed to serve as infantry support units. The 3rd Tank Regt, AA Regt, and Engineering Regt entered Korea on May 30, 1951, and saw action in June in support of the 39th and 43rd Armies; they claimed two tank kills and one damaged, but were almost wiped out. The 3rd Tank Regt left Korea in 1952 and was replaced by 4th Tank Regt, which was assigned to support the 23rd and 38th Armies. (T-34 tank No.215 claimed five tank kills and one damaged, and was additionally credited with destroying 26 bunkers, nine artillery pieces and one truck; honored as a "People's Hero Tank," it is currently on display at the Tank Museum in Běijīng.)

In order to gain combat experience, both the motorized infantry and mobile artillery regiments of the 2nd Armd Div were deployed to Korea on February 15, 1953, and served as mobile defense units to guard China's supply route into Korea. In May 1953 they were ordered to the front to support the 23rd and 24th Armies during the Battle of Seoul. The AA Regt returned to China during 1954, and the Mobile Arty Regt that December. On the conclusion of the Korean War the Mot Inf Regt took on elements of 13 companies from units of the 12th, 20th, and 57th Armies to reconstitute its strength, and the whole division was placed under the command of Jǐnán MR in 1955. By **1958** the 2nd Armd Div had under command the 3rd and 4th Tank Regts, now wholly equipped with the T-34/85; the now-Mechanized Inf Regt, with three infantry battalions and a T-34 tank battalion; a tank training battalion, and a Mot Arty Regt with three battalions of 122mm guns.

In July **1963** the 3rd Tank Regt received 80x Type 59 tanks. With the deterioration of Sino-Soviet relations in the late 1960s and a major PLA expansion in anticipation of an all-out war, many experienced cadres were transferred to be used as the basis of new units. In **1969** the 3rd and 4th Tank Regts and the Mot Arty Regt were redesignated the 5th, 6th and 7th Tank Regts, and the 7th received its Type 59s in 1971.

In February **1976**, Nos.1 and 2 Cos of the tank battalion of the Mech Inf Regt were transferred out to form the basis of the new Armored Troops & Political Cadre School of the CMC. At the same time No.3 Co was assigned to form the Armor Technical College. The 2nd Armd Div was transferred from Jǐnán to Nánjīng MR in **1978**; it sent 110 officers and 1,579 troops to the 1979 Sino-Vietnamese War.

Under Dèng Xiǎopíng's reforms introduced from 1985, the 2nd Armd Div was allocated to 12th Group Army. During the second wave of personnel cuts in **1988** the Mech Inf Regt was disbanded and its equipment distributed to surviving regiments. In June 1989, personnel from 2nd Co, Recon Bn and the Communications Bn were airlifted into Běijīng to help quell civil unrest during the Tiananmen Square episode, and the rest of the division were assigned "police" duties in and around the Xúzhōu area.

Today, still part of the Nánjīng MR and under command of 12th Group Army, the 2nd Armd Div is equipped with the Type 96G MBT.

Tank crew in 1949, wearing Soviet-style padded helmets; clearly visible on the turret of the captured Japanese tank is the yellow-rimmed red star with the yellow characters "8.1."

The Type 59 II tank introduced in 1984 was based on the Type 59 I, but fitted with a 105mm rifled gun based on the British L7 technology, and an improved radio.

Armor

In 1949 the total PLA tank force was only 375 AFVs, mostly Japanese Type 97s, US Stuart light tanks and amphibious LVT Water Buffalos. Company strength was just seven tanks (two per platoon plus one for the company commander), and a battalion could muster only 23 tanks. With Soviet aid, this force was increased to 10 regiments equipped with the T-34/85, JS-2 and SU-122; and by 1955 another 47 regiments had been added, for a total 3,030 all-Soviet tanks. In 1959 China was able to produce its own first tank, a copy of the T-54 designated Type 59. However, due to the disruption of the Cultural Revolution in the 1960s–70s the build-up of the armor force was slow. A regiment had 40–50 tanks; each tank division had 266 Type 59s and 20–30 Type 63 light tanks, and the whole PLA inventory had a shortfall of some 2,200 tanks. Until the late 1980s the PLA had essentially a tank-only force with virtually no other types of AFV. By 1980 there were 10,000 Type 59s, but only 2,000 APCs and some 700 ARVs; in the 1979 Sino-Vietnamese War the PLA could field only one armored MBRL battalion.

Since 1980 and the classification of units as Class A or Class B, formations deployed in Northern China to meet the Soviet threat have traditionally been tank-heavy, with as many as six regiments per Class A division. From 1985 independent tank regiments were all concentrated into the group armies. On paper a battalion had 40–41 tanks and a regiment 150 MBTs, but actual tank strength was much lower: only 31 per battalion (in three 10-tank

The latest Chinese MBT is the ZTZ-99, armed with a 125mm smoothbore gun. Due to its high unit cost only small numbers were built, and these are deployed mainly in the Shěnyáng and Běijīng Military Regions.

Three PAP sniper-school students photographed wearing Model 07 "digital" camouflage clothing; under magnification they can be seen to wear Model 87 PAP collar patches. The 5.8mm QBU-88 rifle issued to both PLA and PAP specialists is not a true sniper's weapon, but the equivalent of a Western "designated marksman's" rifle.

companies plus a single-tank HQ), 93 for a regiment, and 290 for a tank division – including 11 light tanks from the divisional recon company. This compared badly with the Soviet tank division of the same era, with 324–334 tanks.

PLA Special Forces

The PLA has a tradition of stealth operations. During the Korean War, and particularly the 1979 Sino-Vietnamese War, special commando groups conducted numerous raids behind enemy lines, carrying out sabotage, kidnapping and LRRPs. Prior to 1988 the PLA would select capable soldiers for special missions, but never formalized these into special forces units. By the late 1980s a shift in military doctrine, from "People's War" to "Local War under high-tech conditions," was already in progress, and this shift was accelerated when the 1991 Gulf War demonstrated that the PLA was outdated by comparison with Western armies. The first Special Force (originally, Rapid Reaction Unit) was formed in Guǎngzhōu MR, and they soon proliferated to every Military Region in China.

PLA Special Forces are more akin to British Royal Marine Commandos or US Rangers than to the SAS and SEALs. They do focus on special reconnaissance and direct-action missions, but also have CT and security roles

in airborne operations. Organized in units with 1,000-plus personnel, they are equipped with the best China can buy. Like their counterparts around the world they place an emphasis on superior physical fitness and small-arms proficiency. All PLA SF units are trained in martial arts and airborne operations, and elements within each unit have specialized training in one or more of the following areas: use of unmanned aerial vehicles, amphibious operations, demolitions, communications, computer skills, and foreign languages. The Ground Forces, PLA/N and PAP each have their own integral special forces. Prior to the Gulf Anti-Piracy Patrol, where PLA/N SF were first deployed, the only opportunities for the public to see Chinese SF in action have been international SF competitions, in which the PLA and PAP SF have achieved impressive results.

The special distinction of the qualified Chinese SF soldier is a coveted black beret. He may also be equipped with some weapons that are not normally seen in regular units. These include the QSW-67 and QSW-06 silenced pistols, QCW-05 silenced submachine gun, crossbow, tranquilizer dart gun, and the unique 7.62mm QSB-91 pistol dagger. Today the PLA Ground Forces have 11 SF Groups, known as TZBD (Tūzhǒng Bùduì, "Special Force"). Each MR has its own SF Group, each with its own name and insignia, and additional SF units are based in the Xinjiang and Tibetan Military Sub-Regions. Some known SF units are:

Běijīng Military Region – "Excalibur of the East" SF (Dōngfāng Shénjiàn); claimed to be 3,000 strong, with sea/land/air capability.

Jǐnán MR – "Black Beret" SF & "Eagle" SF (Hēibèiléi & Xióngyīng Tūzhǒng Bùduì). Nothing is known about the former; the latter specializes in sea/land/air recon operations.

Shěnyáng MR – "Tiger of the Northeast" SF (Dōngběi Měnghǔ TZBD); marine specialists, with emphasis on underwater direct-action operations.

Nánjīng MR – "Flying Dragon" SF (Fēilóng TZBD); founded in 1992, and

G **SPECIAL & AIRBORNE FORCES**
(1) Major, Special Forces, 2009
This officer was photographed during a 60th National Day parade, wearing a Special Forces version of the latest "pixelated" camouflage uniform. For the parade he has white gloves; a woven yellow-on-dark-green Model 07 PLA cap badge fixed to his helmet cover; and a special variant of the SF shoulder patch, incorporating a reference to the 60th anniversary in the upper line of characters. His rank is displayed on the usual collar patches. His tactical vest differs from the standard Type 06, and he carries a silenced 5.8mm QCW-05 submachine gun, with its staggered-row 50-round magazine.
(2) Captain, Special Forces, Type 87 camouflage uniform, 1990s
This officer, photographed during the 1990s, wears a Special Forces black beret with Model 87 cap badge, and a lightweight shirt in Type 87 "woodland" pattern camouflage (here fitted with gold buttons for smart barracks dress). The mainly green woodland Type 87 design for temperate climate use was the first standardized mass-issue camouflage pattern in the PLA, and is still the most commonly seen. The captain displays his rank in yellow-on-dark-green "velvet-effect" everyday working-dress shoulder straps, and, on his left arm, a general PLA Special Forces patch incorporating the colors of

the three services. The inclusion of the English word "China" is an example of the more outward-looking policies of the PLA in the past two decades, during which it has raised its international profile by participating in UN operations, and in multinational military exercises and exchanges, which require such identification. A subdued version of this patch is also seen, with black edging, stripe edges, motif and lettering on a drab all-green shield.
(3) Type 99 "urban" camouflage, Airborne Forces
This variant of the woodland pattern camouflage, used by paratroopers, was first seen during the 1999 National Day parade. It remained in use until 2005–06, when it was replaced by a Model 07 "pixelated" pattern. The sleeve patch is the general insignia of the PLA airborne force, commonly seen in the 1990s and early 2000s.
(4) Sleeve patch, Special Forces team for Guangzhou Military Region ("Sword of the South")
(5) Nanjing MR SF team ("Flying Dragon")
(6) Beijing MR SF team ("Excalibur of the East")
(7) Shenyang MR SF team ("Tiger of the Northeast")
(8) 44th Airborne Division
(9) Airborne Special Force. "KJTZ" is the abbreviation for the Pinyin transliteration Kong Jiang ("Airborne") Te Zhong ("Special" – i.e. Special Force). This unit is believed to be under command of 43rd Airborne Division.

Close-up of the PAP's distinctive version of the Model 07 "digital" camouflage uniform. The collar patches with two bars and four stars identify a senior colonel. For the "winged" breast badge, see Plate H2b.

claimed to have a major CT role. In a notable exercise conducted in 1997 in full view of the media, the "Flying Dragon" SF carried out an airplane hostage rescue combining use of unmanned aerial vehicles, a helicopter strike force and hostage-rescue teams.

Guǎngzhōu MR – "Sword of Southern China" SF (Huánán Zhījiàn TZBD); founded in 1988, and claimed to be 4,000-strong, with extensive sea/land/air capability. This unit was cross-trained with PLA/N and PLA/AF to specialize in amphibious operations; 400 members are said to be trained marine-vessel operators and pilots.

Chéngdū MR – "Cheetah of the Southwest" SF (Xīnánlièbào TZBD). This is an area of high mountain plateaux and forests, and the SF troops of this MR are skilled mountaineers highly trained for cold-weather operations.

Lánzhōu MR – "Sirius" SF (Tiānláng Tūjīduì). Lánzhōu is close to Yánān, traditionally a PLA stronghold since the 1940s anti-Japanese campaign. The founding father of Chinese SF, Gen Péng Xuěfēng, created a force known as the Xuěfēng (Snowy Maple) Regt, also nicknamed "Tiger" or "Night Tiger" Regt on account of their fighting skills and stealthy movement. This tradition continued to the year 2000, when Sirius SF Group was formed from the nucleus of No. 8 Special Tactics Co of the Xuěfēng (184th) Regt. Each member of the SF is required to be cross-trained and qualified in a number of skills – parachuting, mountaineering, swimming, driving, and hand-to-hand combat – and to be proficient with at least six types of weapon.

PAP "Snow Leopard" Commando Unit

The "Snow Leopard" Commando Unit (Xuěbào Tūjīduì) is the PAP's premier CT force, controlled by the Běijīng PAP Garrison special operations command. Founded in 2002 in reaction to the New York "9/11" attacks the previous year, its existence was only revealed to the public in 2006 as part of China's commitment to the 2008 Olympics. Officially part of the 3rd Regt, 13th Detachment of the Běijīng PAP Garrison, it was first nicknamed "Snow Wolf" but was renamed in 2007. The best equipped and most capable PAP SF team, it has participated in a number of highly visible operations, and is recognized nationwide. Although based in Běijīng the SLCU has a national role, and should not be confused with the local Běijīng Police SWAT team. The SLCU consists of four squadrons with specific responsibilities: 9th and 10th Sqns are CT specialists, 11th is a bomb disposal squadron, and 12th Sqn provide snipers.

From 2003 onward selected individuals from Běijīng PAP SF Bn 5th Detachment were deployed to Iraq for VIP and embassy protection. The Chinese press reported that an SLCU detachment was also deployed to Kabul, Afghanistan in 2008 and 2009.

Airborne Force

In 1950 the PLA/AF got its own ground force with the establishment of its 1st Ground Combat Bde, formed from elements of the 89th Div from 30th Army. At first in Shanghai, the brigade HQ later moved to Kāifēng. Upgraded to divisional and later army status, it had several name changes – to the 1st Parachute Div, then 1st Airborne Div, and, in May 1961, to 15th Airborne Army (to honor the 15th Army's illustrious battle record in Korea). In October 1964 a PLA/AF transport regiment was created to support the airborne force, and in 1969 a helicopter regiment was added. The 13th Transport Div of the PLA/AF is now permanently assigned to the airborne army, with an airlift regiment of about 25–30 aircraft allocated to each of

The PLA's paratroopers were first seen in public during the National Day parade in 1951. They wear Soviet-style padded jump-helmets and carry Type 54 submachine guns, and for the parade they have laid aside their chest-mounted reserve packs.

PLA/AF paratroopers of 15th Airborne Army marching in the 2009 National Day parade. They wear an Airborne "blues" version of Model 07 digital camouflage uniform with Type 03 PCG, and are armed with the folding-stock QBZ-03 assault rifle.

the three divisions. Currently PLA/AF airlift capacity is only sufficient to lift one division – of *c*.11,000 men including supporting arms – at a time, but it can be supplemented with civilian aircraft and utility transports. The PLA can move a regiment of paratroopers with light armored vehicles to anywhere within China in less than 24 hours.

The formation went through several force reductions, notably in 1975 and 1985. In the 1990s the change of military doctrine boosted the RRU concept, and 15th Abn Army benefited by an increase of 25 percent in its strength. In 1993 the formation was transferred from the control of Guǎngzhōu MR to become the strategic reserve and RRU of the Central Military Commission. Today, still part of the PLA/AF, the 15th Abn Army is China's primary rapid reaction formation.

Nicknamed "The Sword of the Blue Sky" (Lántiān Lìjiàn), it was reformed in 2001, with Army HQ located in Xiàogǎn. The 15th Abn Army is composed of three airborne divisions, each about 10,000 strong. The 43rd Abn Div, in Kāifēng, has 127th and 128th Abn MRs Regts, and 129th Abn Arty Regiment. Both 44th and 45th Abn Divs are located around Wǔhàn City; the 44th Div has the 130th Regt (unit type unknown) and 131st Abn Arty Regt, and the 45th Div the 132nd Abn Arty Regt, 133rd Regt (unit type unknown)

The latest air-droppable IFV is the ZBD-03, armed with a 30mm gun and coaxial 7.62mm MG, and a launcher rail for the HJ-73C ATGM. Based on the Ukrainian K/STW-17 BPS system, the ZBD-03 has four large parachute packs mounted on top of the vehicle, and for the drop it rides on a platform with eight large air bags to cushion the landing. It is reported in the Chinese press that the vehicle can be driven off the drop zone 10 minutes 30 seconds after touching down.

and 134th Abn MRs Regiment. The airborne army also has integrated artillery, air defense, recon, engineer, chemical defense, communications, and logistics units. The 43rd Abn Div has a subordinate Special Operations Group, while the 44th provides the training depot for all new recruits.

Paratroopers are recruited throughout China by special teams; new recruits are generally between the ages of 18 and 20 and most are junior high school graduates. They enlist for a minimum of four years, and may stay for up to six years. Those who want to remain in the Army as a career must be selected as NCO or officer material. Junior officers assigned to the parachute force receive their basic officer commission at the military academy, and then transfer to the parachute depot for airborne training. A notable deployment of the PLA's airborne force occured during the 2008 Sichuan earthquake emergency, including an operational jump by 15 pathfinders to survey the damage at first hand. The use of paragliders is common within the airborne force.

Strategic strike force: Second Artillery Corps

The Second Artillery Corps (SAC, Dìèr Pàobīng Bùduì) is China's strategic missile force, controlling nuclear and conventional ballistic weapons. As such it answers to the CMC directly, and operationally to the GSD. The PLA had a missile force as far back as 1959, but when China gained its first atomic bomb in 1964 the conventional missile force was transformed, and renamed as the Second Artillery Corps at the instigation of the Chinese premier Zhōu Ēnlái. The SAC was established on July 1, 1966, but remains a secretive organization; it only made its first public appearance at the National Day parade in October 1984.

With headquarters in Qīnghé near Běijīng, the SAC comprises 90,000–120,000 personnel in six ballistic missile divisions and various supporting elements. These include the early warning division, a communications regiment, a security regiment, and assorted technical support units. The Corps also operates a dedicated Command College in Wǔhàn to prepare officers for senior roles within the SAC; an Engineering College in Xī'ān for technical staff; a design academy; and four research institutes, each handling a different aspect of the use of strategic missiles. The six divisions are

China's latest land attack cruise missile is the CJ-10, a development of the Russian Kh-55; its estimated range is 1,500–2,500km (930–1,525 miles).

The DF-31A is a road-mobile, three-stage, long-range, solid-propellant ICBM that can carry a single 1,000-kiloton thermonuclear warhead. It is operated by the SAC's 812th and 813th Guided Missile Launcher Brigades. The vehicle seen here in the foreground, resembling a "Hummer," is the latest Dōng Fēng Měng Shì ("East Wind Warrior").

independently deployed in Military Regions, but answer directly to SAC HQ rather than to the relevant MR HQ. Each division has a training team, and a maintenance unit for nuclear warheads (commonly referred to in the Chinese press as "special equipment"). Attached to each division are regiment-sized specialist units responsible for chemical defense, communications, training, security, and weather. The SAC divisions, consisting of deployed Guided Missile Launcher Brigades, are each headed by a major general. The GMLB is headed by a senior colonel, and has up to four launch battalions – all generally equipped with one type of missile only, to facilitate maintenance and logistics.

Recruits on a training march. Dressed in green cold-weather training uniforms, they still have the old-fashioned chest webbing, and are loaded down with the large Model 01 pack. The red sleeve patch is a semi-official unit distinction.

According to the Chinese press, the PLA has six operational missile bases, numbered from 51st to 56th. Four of these (51st, 52nd, 55th and 56th) are "Army-level" units, while the 53rd and 54th are "Sub-Army level." There is also an Army-level Training & Experimental Base, numbered the 22nd.

PERSONNEL
Recruitment and training
China operates a selective conscription system, the number of new recruits needed being determined annually by the GSD and GPD. These manpower demands are then issued to each MR, with quotas for each MSD to fill, to include both the PLA and PAP. In November of each year potential recruits are notified, and then undergo physical and political tests. If they pass, they are issued with uniforms and a travel order to report to the training regiments in groups. Units receiving new soldiers will have established reception committees to help the recruits settle in. Division and brigade commanders and political officers are responsible for basic training, to be conducted according to the standards set. Selected officers and NCOs from the division

These fully-trained soldiers wear the latest QGF-03 helmet and Model 07 "digital" camouflage combat uniform with Type 95 Personal Combat Gear, and carry the 5.8mm QBZ-95 rifle. Behind each soldier's right hip is a gas-mask satchel in the older "woodland" pattern camouflage. The patrol leader in front is a lieutenant. (Author's photo)

conduct recruit training; recruits are grouped into squads each headed by a JNCO, these squads into platoons and platoons into companies. Basic training lasts about three months, generally over the coldest winter period. Conscripts are not allowed to marry, and must stay in barracks throughout the period of their service.

At the end of training, the new soldiers are given insignia and rank and take the "Soldier's Oath," raising the clenched right fist; the oath is read out by the group while looking at the PLA flag or Army Badge. The oath has gone through a number of changes; the latest version, promulgated in June 2010, can be translated thus: *"I am a member of the PLA. I promise that I will follow the leadership of the CCP, serve the people wholeheartedly, obey orders, strictly observe discipline, fight heroically, fear no sacrifice, work hard, practice hard to master combat skills, and be ready for combat at all times. Under no circumstances will I betray the PLA, and I will defend the Motherland until my death."*

After basic training, soldiers are assigned to their permanent units for additional training. Special skills and technical training include driving, radios, artillery, chemical defense, and so forth. Previously those recruits with special ability were quickly identified and selected to become potential JNCOs, but as the PLA moves toward becoming a professional force this practice is being abandoned, and JNCOs are selected from volunteers and ex-conscripts who sign on as professional soldiers.

Conscription normally lasts for two years; the first-year soldier is termed a private (Lièbīng), and in the second year he is promoted to private first class (Shǎngděng Bīng). Pay is dependent on rank and years in service, with supplements given to those serving in hardship conditions such as desert or snowy mountain regions. In November of their second year those who do not want to sign on as career soldiers are demobilized and return home. Some de-mobbed soldiers may be required to serve in the Reserves or Militia.

The NCOs

In 1999 the PLA decided to move toward a Western model, and announced a cut in the term of conscription to two years; this was accompanied by a decision to increase the number of non-coms and give them greater responsibilities. NCOs (Shìguān) are normally selected from capable volunteers at the end of their conscription period, but some are enlisted directly from civilian life on account of their specialist technical knowledge or skills. (In 2003, 630 NCOs were recruited in this way; in 2004 that number increased to 1,064, including 300 female NCOs.) The NCOs are divided into six grades, and may stay on active duty for 30 or more years, up to the age of 55. Ranks and required lengths of service for each grade are as follows:

Junior NCOs – Grades 1 and 2, both requiring a minimum service of three years.

Intermediate NCOs – Grades 3 and 4, both requiring at least four years' service.

Senior NCOs – Grade 5 NCOs require a minimum of five years' service, and Grade 6 require a minimum nine-year contract.

Prospective NCO candidates must submit a written application and be recommended by their unit and political officers. After taking an exam in January, those accepted report to academies for two or more years' training. Should NCOs wish to extend their initial contracts they must repeat the same approval process. Promotions are approved at division or brigade level for Grade 3 and 4 NCOs, and at army level for Grades 5 and 6. They are encouraged to continue their professional education, either through correspondence courses or attendance at military or civilian institutions. The grading of NCOs' performance is uniquely Chinese: besides recommendation by their superior officers, they are also evaluated by the soldiers in their unit, so the opinions of the ordinary soldiers do count.

NCOs may marry, but they are required to live in barracks. In most cases their spouses are allowed to visit them once a year, staying in quarters inside the garrison for up to 45 days, although the families of approved SNCOs are authorized to live with them in barracks. The PLA now expects its NCOs to be capable of taking on more responsibilities. There is a movement to replace supply/logistic officers (Sīwù Zhǎng) with SNCOs, and SNCOs are increasingly expected to command operations, organize training, and manage subordinates.

The officers

Promotion from the rank-and-file has been the traditional source of officers for the PLA, but as modern warfare puts ever-greater demands on technical skills increasing numbers of new PLA officers are being recruited from among graduates of civilian colleges and universities, alongside cadets from military universities and personnel selected from the enlisted ranks. The PLA sponsors promising students through higher education under the management of Reserve Officer Selection & Training Offices in the universities; they are required to attend military training during the holiday periods whilst at university, and to join the PLA upon graduation. Secondary or high school

graduates continue to be the main source of officers, however, and cadet entry into military academies is increasingly popular. Applicants for military academies must be under 20 years old, unmarried, and physically and politically qualified. Tuition is provided by the government, and cadets are paid modest sums while attending the academy.

PLA academies

These institutes provide both university-level education and basic military training to prepare cadets for assignment to operational units immediately after graduation. Currently there are approximately 35 schools offering four-year courses; graduating cadets receive a bachelor's degree and are commissioned as second lieutenants. Academies are subordinate to the various systems overseen by the four General Headquarters Departments. Many PLA institutions at all levels offer advanced degrees, and the PLA also sends officers to civilian universities, both in China and abroad. A much smaller number of intermediate-level academies, termed Command Academies, train serving mid-level officers from battalion to division

The Model 07 uniform PLA Army officer's peaked cap. Officers are classified by their ranks, duty appointments and career categories. There are ten officer ranks, in three grade levels (company, field and general) similar to Western structures; on average, an officer is promoted approximately every four years if he has passed the required exams. Today, duty appointments are divided into 15 levels, from platoon commander up to chairman of the CMC. Categories are classified as operational, political, logistic, ordnance, and technical officers. For the most part, once officers are categorized into the system they do not transfer out of their specialties unless they are promoted to general rank. (Author's photo)

level. Like many staff colleges in Western armies that accept students from friendly countries, the PLA's Nánjīng Army Command Academy also has a Foreign Training Dept which is attended by officers from many different armies. At the top of the PLA professional education pyramid are the NDU and NUDT (see above, "Senior-level academies").

Uniformed civilian personnel

The PLA also includes civilians who, despite wearing uniforms, do not hold military ranks. PLA civilians are categorized as specialist technical cadres, non-specialist technical cadres, and office or administrative personnel. PLA civilians may acquire officer status after completing the required training, and likewise PLA officers who have reached retirement age may become civilian employees and stay within the PLA system.

UNIFORMS & COMBAT EQUIPMENT

PLA uniforms

Two soldiers wearing Model 65 uniform and FK-80 helmets crew a 7.62mm Type 57 heavy machine gun in hill country during the mid-1980s fighting on the Vietnamese border.

Before 1950 the PLA was essentially still a guerrilla army equipped with a variety of civilian or captured clothing. Often soldiers wore old Nationalist uniforms with badges removed and replaced with a red star, and/or a cloth tab over the left breast pocket printed with the words "China People's Liberation Army." The uniform of this era was often a sand-colored padded cotton jacket with four pockets, and a "Máo cap" with an attached red star

badge bordered in yellow. In January 1950, the tri-service PLA got its first official military uniform code, known to the world as **Model 50** uniform. This was the official dress from January 4, 1950 to September 30, 1955; and it was in this uniform that the PLA went into the Korean War, albeit with all insignia removed. It appeared in various shades of yellowish-green and drab green, with quilted jackets and trousers and fleece-lined caps for winter use.

The introduction of the **Model 55** uniform was part of the great reform of the PLA, which included a new look, the first military pay structure, a professional career system, and a new system of awards and decorations. The 1950s were the Sino-Soviet honeymoon period, when the PLA received Soviet weapons and embraced Soviet-style uniform and insignia (see Plate A). For the first time different types of uniforms were also introduced for winter and summer, working and formal dress, and even combat dress with subdued badges. Features included Soviet-style "Sam Browne" belts for officers, *ushanka* caps and large overcoats for winter, peaked (visored) caps for officers and sidecaps for enlisted ranks, with Soviet-style cavalry trousers and boots for the armored corps.

In 1958 there was a minor revision to the Model 55 uniforms; **Model 58** officers' rank insignia were now to be placed on the collar patches instead of

The transitional Model 85 regulations introduced peaked caps for the service dress uniforms of all ranks. The officers' cap (top) had a red band and silver chin cords, the enlisted ranks' cap a plain green band and black chinstrap. Note the Model 85 cap badge; this changed again in 1987.

on Soviet-style shoulder boards. As Sino-Soviet relations increasingly soured, the **Model 60** uniform continued to lose obvious elements of Soviet styling; for example, the badge for the Transport Corps, previously modeled on a Soviet GAZ truck, was even changed to show a Chinese-made "Liberation" truck. During the 1960s the advent of the Cultural Revolution and Leftist thinking ushered in a period of Revolutionary puritanism. Stripped of all rank insignia and badges, the **Model 65** uniform was just a green "Máo suit" with a simple red star cap badge and plain red collar patches (see Plate B). The only way to distinguish between officers and soldiers was that officers' jackets had four pockets and soldiers' only two breast pockets. In 1974 Máo approved some minor deviations from the strict Model 65, which were incorporated in the **Model 74** uniform.

From 1978 China began to reopen its doors to the world and introduce a series of economic reforms. After the bitter experience of the 1979 war with Vietnam, when a "rankless" army proved to be a disaster, in 1980 the CMC announced the reintroduction of military ranks. As a temporary measure before their full-scale reintroduction, from 1985 to 1988 the **Model 85** uniform was worn. Most noticeably, peaked caps appeared for all ranks, with bands in red, black or royal blue and silver chin cords for officers of the three services. Jacket collars bore patches in these colors, outlined yellow for officers, though with a single star pin for all ranks; and badges of the three services were worn on plain shoulder boards in olive green, dark blue and royal blue. Significantly, the Chinese characters "8.1" reappeared in the middle of the red star on the cap badge; this acquired an anchor for the PLA/N and wings for the PLA/AF, almost returning to a Model 55 look. Winter and summer uniforms were redesigned, the latter replacing the jacket with an open-neck, short-sleeved shirt worn over the trousers, and for the first time in many years skirts were worn by female soldiers.

After a hiatus of 23 years, in 1987 the CMC formally reintroduced military ranking into the PLA and PAP (see Plate D). The **Model 87** uniforms included for the first time (from October 1, 1988) an elaborate system of insignia for four grades of JNCOs, as well as SNCOs. Ranks were displayed on the shoulder straps using slides, and on Soviet-style shoulder boards for

BELOW LEFT
The original 1997 shoulder patch for the Hong Kong Garrison; see Plate E1 & E2.

BELOW RIGHT
The redesigned Hong Kong Garrison shoulder patch for Model 07 uniform; compare with Plate F4. This combination of yellow script, star and branches with gray crossed rifles on a dull green ground is the basic design of all such patches.

officers' dress uniforms. All ranks wore peaked caps, or in extreme cold weather the *ushanka*. For the first time uniforms and headdress with badges for civilian employees of the PLA were introduced; while displaying no ranks, their shoulder straps bore a badge identifying one of the three services. Other innovations included special designs for the National Honor Guard, PLA bands and the Entertainment Regiment. Members of the honor guard for each of the three services had an elaborate uniform in their unique colors, with double-striped trousers tucked into high cavalry-style boots, and large golden-yellow aiguillettes hanging from the left shoulder. The military bands and entertainers had somewhat similar uniforms but with their own shoulder boards. The Model 87 uniforms were worn for longer than the now-conventional ten-year period, and the shoulder rank insignia worn with dress and working uniforms saw several successive changes in 1992 and 1993.

A recent addition to Model 07 uniform is this National Defense Badge, worn above the left breast pocket by personnel on active duty. This Ground Forces version represents the army's red-over-green flag, replaced in the PAP version by the PRC national flag. (Author's photo)

The **Model 97** uniform was a short-term experiment in a style created for the new PLA Hong Kong Garrison, which included yet another sequence of shoulderboard insignia for line and technical NCOs. It was intended to extend the Model 97 uniform to the rest of the army in 2000, but due to high cost only limited numbers of the PLA received it. Consequently, until the arrival of the Model 07 the rest of the army had to make do with the Model 87 uniform. To extend its life minor modifications were made in 1999, 2004 and 2005, incorporating a new summer dress and working dress as a stopgap measure. The most prominent features of the Model 97 uniform regulations were the introduction of berets, of NCOs' chevrons replacing bars on shoulder rank slides, and of some formation shoulder patches (see Plate E). To complete the new look, the open-collar Model 97 uniform included metal collar and breast badges denoting the three services, as well as US-style name tabs.

The **Model 07** is the current uniform for the PLA and PAP (see Plate H). Unveiled in late June 2007 during the ceremony celebrating the tenth anniversary of the transfer of sovereignty over Hong Kong, this new uniform began to replace both the updated Model 87, and the Model 97 then in use by garrison troops in Hong Kong and Macau. Compared to the previous brownish "olive green" service uniforms in use since the mid-1980s, the new Ground Forces Model 07 uniforms feature a colder "pine green" color, with better material and tailoring to give a more stylish appearance. Each PLA serviceman has a winter combat and training uniform made of woollen material, and a summer combat and training uniform made of polycotton twill fabric; these consist of a jacket, trousers, and soft cap, worn with black leather boots. All rank insignia are displayed in yellow on dark green collar patches. The old standing-collar winter service jacket was definitively abandoned in favor of an open-collar design worn with shirt and necktie. Other features are a new cap badge, a new service cap for female personnel,

A female soldier of the Hong Kong Garrison in Model 07 uniform, summer shirtsleeve order – compare with Plate H3. Note the rank slides on the shoulder straps, with the single yellow chevron of a Grade 1 JNCO; the plain wreathed-star collar badges; and, on her right breast, the woven PLA Ground Forces badge (see Plate F3). This photo was taken on the PLA's open day in October 2011 when, for security reasons, all personnel were instructed to remove for the day the name tag normally worn above the left pocket. (Author's photo)

a British-style woollen pullover, the introduction of a rank grade for cadets, and a simplified ranking structure for NCOs. Overall the uniform is much more colorful, with a liberal expansion in the use of formation shoulder patches (37 different examples at the time of writing), metal and woven breast badges, name tabs, national flag patches, and medal-style breast ribbons indicating length of of service and present appointment.

People's Armed Police

Throughout the decades the PAP has followed the PLA with a similar pattern of uniforms, though with minor variations. During the 1960s the PAP wore the same plain Model 65 uniform and cap badge. In 1974 and in 1983 a new cap badge and a new shoulder strap badge were introduced; otherwise there was no difference between PAP and PLA uniform. As in the PLA, ranks reappeared with the introduction of the Model 87 uniforms. Today a new cap badge, rank slides and a large PAP shoulder patch are the major points of differentiation between the PAP and PLA. A new NCO rank structure came into being in 1993, expanding the previous six grades to 12, but these were reduced again to seven grades in 1997. Like those of the PLA, the PAP Model 87 uniforms were revised in 2001, 2004 and 2005 during the long wait for a new PAP Model 07 uniform to come into use (see Plate H).

Combat dress and equipment

In 1979 the PLA troops marching into Vietnam still wore plain green uniforms, although some elite troops had been illustrated earlier wearing camouflage clothing in a four-color "DPM"-style pattern. In *c.*1984 reversible camouflage uniforms made their first appearance, with a "woodland" pattern on the primary side and a spotted "duck-hunter" pattern on the inside (see Plate C). The "duck-hunter" camouflage proved to be unpopular and was soon dropped; for almost 20 years thereafter the PLA used only four-color "woodland"-style camouflage patterns for its three

Soldiers photographed on the PLA's open day in 2011 wearing daily working dress of a soft fatigue cap, jacket and trousers in "digital" pattern camouflage, and the latest plastic-clip pistol belt. Note woven cap badge and Ground Forces right breast badge. These soldiers are lined up to man a rifle range for the public, with QBZ-95 rifles fitted with laser-emitter training devices. (Author's photo)

services – the definitive model being the Type 87 (see Plate G2) – though with several variations in color combinations. Those that have been illustrated include a tan-based "arid" or desert-and-mountain pattern; a gray-dominated "urban" pattern; a "winter" pattern; a "woodland" variation issued to the SAC in densely forested regions; and finally, a blue-dominated "ocean" pattern issued to Navy special units and marines. For day-to-day work the PLA soldier may wear a camouflage-pattern soft field cap or, in more formal dress codes, a peaked cap or beret with his combat clothing.

On October 1, 2009 China celebrated the 60th National Day with massive military parades, and on this occasion several new computer-generated "digital" or "pixelated" patterns of camouflage clothing were seen

中 国 武 警
雪 豹 突 击 队
北 京

Chinese characters: first line, "China People's Armed Police" **(see Plate H1c & 3a)**; second line, "Snow Leopards Commandos" **(see H1c)**; third line, "Beijing" **(see H2b)**.

H PEOPLE'S ARMED POLICE

(1) Senior NCO, "Snow Leopard" Commandos; Iraq, 2008
This special-force policeman, armed with the QBZ-95 rifle, is dressed in a Type 05 PAP "pixelated" camouflage uniform (since replaced with an 07 pattern). His Model 07 yellow-on-dark green collar patches **(see 1a)** show the crossed rifles on a wreath and two thick chevrons identifying a Grade 4 SNCO. The same yellow insignia are displayed on red shoulder boards, just visible under his black tactical vest. The yellow-on-green PAP shoulder patch (not his unit patch) is worn on his right sleeve **(see 3a)**. Since he is serving overseas – on embassy protection duty – a national flag/"China" patch is worn on the left sleeve, above a "China" title in the local language, Arabic **(see 1b)**; the flag patch is repeated on his tactical vest.
(1c) "Snow Leopard" Commando Unit sleeve patch. Note the small bottom title line in English

(2) Lieutenant, Model 07 dress uniform
This junior officer wears the PAP Model 07 uniform in the PLA's new "pine green," embellished for a formal occasion with a white plastic "Sam Browne" belt. His shoulder-board rank insignia of two gold stars on a gold stripe are in PLA style, but he has the distinctive PAP collar insignia – a gold star, on a gold-rimmed shield of red over dark blue, in the angle of a spray of gold leaves. The leaves also appear on the peak of his cap; this has yellow piping at the crown seam, green chin cords, and the PAP cap badge. The PAP sleeve patch **(3a)** is

in this case worn on the left arm. On his right breast he wears a "winged" bi-metal badge showing his current assignment – here, Beijing – above the Roman letters "CAPF" for Chinese Armed Police Force **(see 2b)**. Below this he wears a white-on-black plastic name tag, again in bilingual form **(see 2c)**. The ribbons above his left breast pocket indicate (left & right) two and five years' service, for a total of seven years; and (center) his current appointment – here, gold cloth with a gold star, indicating a deputy staff officer.
(2a) PAP cap badge, pre-2000
The Model 07 version (seen on **H2** & **H3**) shows the central shield within a wreath extended upwards to enclose it completely (compare with PLA badge on **page 4**).

(3) Female captain, Model 07 summer shirtsleeve uniform
The modern appearance of this officer of the Beijing PAP Garrison epitomizes the reforms of recent decades – the comparison with Plate B1 is striking. She wears a stylish female hat, with a modification of the insignia worn by H2; a short-sleeved summer blouse, a skirt and high-heeled shoes. The collar badges, of a star between leafy branches, are simpler than those of H2, but the flat-woven rank insignia on her shoulder boards are in the usual PLA officer's style. She displays the PAP left sleeve patch **(3a)**; on her right breast is a woven version of the "winged" assignment badge, and her bilingual name tag is pinned above her left pocket.
(3a) PAP sleeve patch

1

2a

2

1a

1b

CHINA
الصين

3

2b

2c
丁　大　中
DING　DA　ZHONG

1c

3a

for the first time (see Plates F & G). These special digital patterns appear in color combinations including a "universal" pattern, a Special Forces type, an "airborne" type used by the PLA/AF 15th Abn Army, and an SAC "woodland" variation.

Chest and waist rigs incorporating magazine and grenade pouches have been in use and waist in one form or another since the 1950s, made in light canvas (see Plates A, B & C). Separate items slung from the shoulders included pouches for LMG drum magazines carried by squad gunners, grenade pouches holding up to four stick grenades, carriers for water canteens and gas masks, and a haversack for personal gear; the slings of all these were usually held

Front and rear views of infantrymen modeling the transformation in the mid-1990s from the old non-integrated personal combat gear to the new Model 95 PCG. The "old-style" soldier (right in the front view, left in the rear view) has chest webbing for four Type 56 "banana magazines" and four Type 55 stick grenades, an aluminum water bottle, gas mask, canvas general-purpose haversack, combat shovel, and blankets tied up with webbing straps (with a spare pair of "liberation shoes" tucked in). By sharp contrast, the "new soldier" has the neatly integrated nylon PCG and, in marching order, a large Bergen-style rucksack.

steady by being passed under a brown leather waist belt. For long-distance combat, the equipment was completed with a backpack without a carrying frame, commonly known in the West as either the "North Vietnamese" or "Chicom" rucksack. For officers, leather pistol holsters and ammo-clip pouches have commonly been attached to the leather belt.

This silhouette did not change until the arrival of the **Type 91 Personal Combat Gear (PCG)**, an integrated chest- and belt-pouch ensemble similar to the US Army's late 1980s Integrated Individual Fighting System (IIFS). Some high-profile units subsequently received **Type 95** and **Type 01** developments of this (see Plate E). As part of the Model 07 uniform, the PLA then introduced a **Type 06 PCG**. This resembles the US MOLLE system, with a vest-like Tactical Assault Panel (TAP) replacing the traditional yoke-and-belt style PCG. In addition the Type 06 PCG has a US-style Pouch Attachment Ladder System (PALS) for varying pouch attachments; the tactical vest can be reinforced with ballistic armor plates, as well as attached throat and groin protectors (see Plate F). To complete the Type 06 PCG the PLA soldier also carries a gas mask, water canteen, NATO-style folding entrenching tool, first aid kit, and multipurpose bayonet.

Outfitting a vast force such as the PLA takes time, and so far only frontline Class A units have been fully equipped with the new gear. Many units – especially Class B formations, training battalions, and reservists – still use a mixture of old and new load-bearing equipment.

Today the PLA is in the process of being equipped with the new QGF-03, a "Fritz"-type helmet made of reinforced ballistic composite material, but the FK-80 steel helmet is still seen, especially in Class B units. Class A units will be equipped with the 5.8mm QBZ-95 assault rifle and Type 06 PCG; a large pack that resembles any modern mountaineering rucksack; and Model 07 combat boots. Class B units using the 5.8mm Type 81 assault rifle (roughly comparable to the Soviet AKM family) are usually issued Type 91 PCG.

The ZBL-92B 6x6 wheeled IFV has a crew of three and can carry nine soldiers. This vehicle serves with the PLA's Hong Kong Garrison. Armament is a ZPT-90 25mm automatic cannon mounted in a one-man turret, and a HJ-73C antitank guided missile launcher, plus a co-axial 7.62mm Type 86 machine gun; 76mm smoke grenade dischargers are mounted on each side of the turret. (Author's photo)

SELECT BIBLIOGRAPHY

English language:

Blasko, Dennis, *The Chinese Army Today* (Routledge, 2006)

Flanagan, Stephen, & Michael Marti (ed.), *The People's Liberation Army and China in Transition* (National Defense University Press, Washington DC, 2003)

Kim Jae Chang, Li or Shih, *The Chinese Military Strategic Culture and Chinese Use of Force during the Cold War* (doctoral thesis, Fetcher School of Law and Diplomacy, 2002)

Lilley, James & David Shambaugh (ed.), *China's Military Faces the Future* (East Gate Books, American Enterprise Institute for Public Policy Research, 1999)

O'Dowd, Edward C., *The Last Maoist War – Chinese Cadres and Conscripts in the Third Indochina War 1978–1991* (doctoral dissertation, Princeton University, 2004)

Qiang Zhang, *China and the Vietnam Wars, 1950–1975* (University of North Carolina Press, Chapel Hill & London, 2000)

Translated titles of Chinese-language works:

Liu Bin Jie et al, *30 Years of Reform of the PLA* (Military Science Publishing, 2008)

Ni Chuang Hui, *Ten Years of Sino-Vietnam War* (M+N Publishing Co, 2010)

Qian Jiang, *The Secret War – The Chinese Military Advisory Group Goes to War in Vietnam* (Henan People's Press, 1992)

Shen Wei Ping & Liu Wen Xiao, *The Battle of Jinmen – Crisis of the Taiwan Straits* (Wings of China Press, 2007)

Wang Zhen Hua et al, *The History of the Chinese Military Advisory Group in the Vietnamese Anti-French War* (PLA Press, 1990)

Wang Zhi Jun, *My Personal Combat Experience in the Sino-Vietnam War 1979* (Thinker Publishing (HK) Limited, 2008)

Xu Ping & Xu Hai Yen, *Expanded Edition: 100 Years of Chinese Military Uniform* (Gold Wall Press, 2009)

Chinese military magazines:

Military History Monthly; Ordnance Industry Science & Technology; Ordnance Knowledge; Small Arms; Tanks & Armored Vehicles; Weapon

INDEX

References to illustrations are shown in **bold**.
Plates are shown with page locators in brackets.

AA units 10, 14, 22, 25, 32, 33, 36, 37, 39:
    weapons 10, 14, **25**, 30, 36
academies/institutes/universities 7, 26–7, 28,
    39, 45, 47, 51–2
administrative personnel 22, **D4(23)**, 32, 34,
    F2b(35), 36, 52
AFVs **12**, 40; air defense units 10, 47
airborne force 42, **G3, 8(43)**, 45–7, **46**
Airborne Special Force 42, **G9(43)**
aircraft 10, 11, 37, 38, 45–6
amphibious ops/units **32**, 33, 39, 42, 44
APCs 11, 12, **24**, 33, 40
armored units 28, **36**, 37, 39
artillery units 8, 14, 22, **25**, 33, **36**, 37, 39, 47:
    weapons 5, 7, 10, 11, 12, 15, 16, 33, **36**, 39, 50
AT units 30, 32, 36: weapons 30, 32, **33**, 36, **46**, 62

ballistic missile divisions 47–8
bayonets 8, **A2(9)**, 12, **B2–3(13)**, 29, 30,
    E3(31), 34, **F1(35)**, 62
border/frontier guard units 18, 21, 24, **25**, 38
businesses, PLA operation of 20

cap badges 4, 8, **A1–2, 7(9)**, 12, **12**,
    B1(13), 18, **C3(19)**, 22, **D1(23)**, 28,
    30, **E1–1a, 2(31)**, 42, **G1–2(43)**, 53,
    55, 56, 57, **57**, 58, **H2, 2a–3a(59)**
Central Military Commission **12**, 14, 20, **21**,
    25, 26, 26, 39, 46, 47, **51**, 54
chemical defense duties/units 25, 47, 48
Chén Gēng, Gen 7, 8, **8**, 10
Chiang Kaishek 4, 5
China Xinjiang Development Group Co. 20
Chinese Civil War 5, 18, 25
Chinese Communist Party 4, 5, **5**, 25, 26
civil aid/development 17, **20**, 22, 25, 47
coastal defense units 21, **25**
commando units **14**, 41: "Snow Leopard"
    45, 58, **58**, **H1, 1c(59)**; "Snow Wolf" 45
communications duties/units 25, 26, 36, 39,
    42, 47, 48
computer/language experts 25, 42
conscription 27, 49, 50
construction/engineering troops 10, 14
counter terrorism specialists 41, 44, 45
Cultural Revolution, impact of on PLA 11–12, **14**,
    15, 40, 54

drivers/driving 8, **A3(9)**, 44, 50

electronic/cyber warfare units 21, 22, 36, 38
embassy protection duties 45, 58, **H1(59)**
engineer units 10, 14, 18, 20, 25, 27, 33,
    36, 39, 47
entertainment troupes 22, **D2–3(23)**, 26, 55
equipment 25, 26: ammo clips/magazines 8,
    A2–3(9), 12, **B3(13)**, 18, **C1, 3(19)**, 29,
    29, 30, 34, **F1–2(35)**, 42, **G1(43)**, 60, 60,
    61; bandoliers 8, **A2(9)**, 29, **29**; gas masks 30,
    60, **60**, 62; PCG 18, **C1, 4(19)**, **28**, 29, 30, **E1,
    3(31)**, 34, **F1–2(35)**, 42, **G1(43)**, 46, 48, 49, 58,
    H1(59), 60–1, 60, 61, 62; pistol cases/holsters
    22, **D1(23)**, 34, **F1–2(35)**, 57, 61; shovels **61**;
    water canteens 12, **B3(13)**, 30, 34, 60, **60**, 62

factories and farms 20, 26, 28, 37
fire-support assets/fire teams 28, 30, 33, 37
forests and gold mines, protection of 24
formation patches (sleeve) 17, 22, 28, 34,
    F2, 4–5(35), 42, **G2–9(43)**, 48, 58, **H1b–1c,
    3–3a(59)**
French Indochina War 7–8, 10

General Headquarters Departments 25, 26,
    27, 34, 51
General Staff Department 22, 26, 38, 47, 49

grenades 11, **14**, 18, **C1(19)**, 29, 30, 34, 60,
    60, 62
Guided Missile Launch Brigades 48
Guō Bóxióng, Gen **26**

helicopter units 38, 44, 45: helicopters 10,
    37, 38, **38**, 44; Ho Chi Minh 7
Honor Guards **17**, 18, **C3(19)**, 28
hospitals 22, 37; hostage-rescue teams 44

IFVs **29**, 32, 33, **46**, **62**
information warfare elements 21
intelligence-gathering 20, 26
internal security units 22, 24, 26

Kuomintang (Nationalist) army 4, 5, **6**, 7
Korean War 6, 7, 8, 10, 18, 39, 45, 53

Lei Feng, Corporal 8, **A3(9)**
Li, Maj **17**; Liáng Guānglie, Gen **21**
local defense duties/forces 21, **25**, 27
logistics units 8, 36, 47, **51**
LSWs 28, 29, **29**; Luo, Col **17**

machine guns 11, **32**: GPMGs **24**;
    HMGs 14, 30, 52, **62**; LMGs 6, 14, 28
"Máo badges/pins" **12**, 8, **A3(9)**, 12,
    B3a(13), 18, **C4(19)**
Máo Zédōng 4, 5, 7, 8, 26, 54
MBRLs 10, 33, 40
medical personnel/teams 12, **B1(13)**, 21, 22,
    D1(23), 32, 36
Military Districts/Police 22, 27, 30, **E2(31)**
Military Regions 25, 33, 37, 38, 47–8, 49:
    Běijīng 27, **27**, **41**, 42, **G6(43)**; Chéngdū
    27, **27**, 34, **F2(35)**, 44; Guǎngzhōu 15,
    27, **27**, 32, 33, 41, 42, **G4(43)**, 44, 46;
    Jǐnán 27, 39, 42; Lánzhōu 27, **27**, 44;
    Nánjīng 27, **27**, 33, 39, 42, **G5(43)**, 44;
    Shanghai **27**; Shěnyáng 27, **27**, 41, 42,
    G7(43)
Military Sub-Districts/-Regions 27, 42, 49
Militia (the) 14, 18, 18, **C4(19)**, 20, 22,
    D1(23), 25, **25**, 50
mines and satchel charges 11, 36
missiles (strategic) *see* Second Artillery Corps
mobilization, preparations for 26, 27
mortar companies/squads 30, 32
mortars 30, 32
motorized units **29**, 33, 36, 37, 39

North Vietnam, border clashes with 7, 14,
    18, **C1–2(19)**; support for 10–11
nuclear weapons 5, 47, 48, **48**

overseas deployments: Afghanistan 45;
    Iraq 45, 58, **H1(59)**

paragliders and UAVs 42, 44, 47
paratroopers 42, **G3(43)**, 45, 46, **46**, 47
PAVN 7, 8, **8**, 10, 14–15, 16
Peng De Huai, Field Marshal 8, **A1(9)**
People's Armed Police 8, 16, 22, **24**, 25, 26,
    58: composition/strength 24, 28, 41, 42,
    45, 56, **H1–3a(57)**; origins 22; ranks 24,
    54, 57; recruitment/training 24, 49; roles
    17, 20, 24, 25, 27; uniforms/insignia 24,
    44, 55–7, 55, 56, 58, **H1–3b(59)**
People's Volunteer Army 6, 7, 8, 10
personnel reductions 5, 16, 39, 50
pistol daggers 42; pistols 22, 34, **F1–2(35)**, 42
PLA Air Force 5, 16, **17**, 21, 34, 38, 39, 44,
    45–7, 50, 54, 60
PLA Ground Force: command echelons 21;
    development and growth 5; emblem/flag
    4, 5, 50, 55, 56; as instrument of the state 4, 18,
    20; military elements of 21; origins of 4, 5;
    remit 20; role in development of PRC 18;
    strength 21; sub-services 20

PLA Navy 16, **17**, 21, 22, 34, 42, 44, 54, 58
PLA Police 8, **A4(9)**
PLA Public Security Army/Troops 22, **24**
political officers 7, 8, 26, 30, 32, 49, 50, **51**
propaganda leaflets/posters 7, **7**, 8
psychological warfare elements 21

radar systems 11; radio operators 30, 32, 36
radios 11, 28, 34, **F2(35)**, 50
Railroad Corps/Ministry 10, 14, 18, 20
rank structures: abolition/return of **14**, 54
"rankless" army, limitations of 54
Rapid Reaction Unit 41, 46
reconnaissance units 32, 36, 39, 41, 42, 47
recruitment and training 11, 24, 26, 36, 37,
    38, 39, 47, 48, 49–52, 62
Red Army of Workers and Peasants 4, 5
Reserve forces 21–2, **22**, **D6–7(23)**, 27, 38,
    50, 51, 62
rifle units/riflemen 28–9, 28, 30, 32
rifles 8, **A2(9)**, 10, 11, 12, **B2–3(13)**, 16,
    17, 18, **C1–4(19)**, 24, 28, **28**, 29, 30,
    E1(31), 32, 34, **F1, 2a(35)**, 36, 41, 46,
    49, 57, 58, **H1(59)**, 62
rocket launcher units 33; rockets (unguided)
    12, 38; RPG teams **12**; RPGs **12**, 28

Second Artillery Corps 21, 34, **F5(35)**, 47–9,
    47, 48, 58, 60
security units 32, 41, 47, 48
Sino-Vietnamese War (1979) 14–16, **14**, 18,
    25, 39, 40, 41
snipers 28, 32, **41**, 45; "Soldier's Oath" 50
Soviet Union, relations with 5, 11–12, **12**,
    B2–3(13), 39, 40–1, 53–4
Special Administrative Regions: Hong Kong
    16, **17**, 27, 27, 30, **E1–2(31)**, 34, 38, 54,
    55, 56, **62**; Macau 16, 27, **27**, 30, 34, **34**,
    F4(35), 50
Special Forces 21, 38, 41–2, **G1–2, 4–7(43)**,
    44, 47, 60
standard guards/standard-bearers **17**
submachine guns 8, **A3(9)**, 42, **G1(43)**, 45
supply/logistics officers 30, 32, 51
survey functions 26; SWAT teams 24

tank units 33, 36, 37, **38**, 39, 40–1
tanks 5, 11, 12, 15, 33, 38, 39, 40–1, **40**, **41**
technical branches/units 27, 32, 47, 50, 52
technical personnel 8, 32, 34, **F2b(35)**, 51, 55
Tiananmen Square, PLA actions 16, 39
Tibet/Tibetan exiles, crushing of revolt 7
transport units 8, 11, 24, 26, 36, 45–6, 54

UN peacekeeping operations 16, 17, **17**, 42
uniforms: Model 05 58, **H1(59)**; Model 07 4,
    17, 22, 26, 30, 34, **F1–5(35)**, 42, **G1(43)**,
    44, 46, 49, 51, 54, 55, 56, 56, 57, 58,
    H2–3(59), 61; Model 55 8, **A1–3, 6(9)**,
    53; Model 58 53–4; Model 60 54;
    Model 65 ("Máo suit") 12, 12, **B1–3(13)**,
    16, 18, **C1, 3(19)**, 52, 54, 56; Model 74
    14, 54; Model 85 22, **D5–6(23)**, 53, 54;
    Model 87 **17**, 21, 22, **D1–4, 7–8(23)**, 30,
    34, 42, **G2(43)**, 54–5, 57, 58; Model 97
    30, **E1–2(31)**, 55; Model 99 42, **G3(43)**

Vietnam, support for 7–8, 10–11; war with
    14–16, **14, 16**, 18, 25, 39, 40, 41, 52, 54
Vietnam War, PLA involvement 10–11
VIP protection/transport 24, 38, 45
Vo Nguyen Giap, Gen 8, **8**

weather units 48; Wéi Guóqīng, Gen 7, 10

Xīnjiāng Production & Construction Corps
    20, **20**

Zhū Dé, Field Marshal 4, 39